Creative Poetry Writing

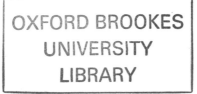

Titles in the Resource Books for Teachers series

Beginners
Peter Grundy

Classroom Dynamics
Jill Hadfield

Creative Poetry Writing
Jane Spiro

Conversation
Rob Nolasco and Lois Arthur

Cultural Awareness
Barry Tomalin and Susan Stempleski

Dictionaries
Jonathan Wright

Drama
Charlyn Wessels

Exam Classes
Peter May

Film
Susan Stempleski and Barry Tomalin

Global Issues
Ricardo Sampedro and Susan Hillyard

Grammar Dictation
Ruth Wajnryb

Homework
Lesley Painter

The Internet
Scott Windeatt, David Hardisty,
and David Eastment

Learner-based Teaching
Colin Campbell and Hanna Kryszewska

Letters
Nicky Burbidge, Peta Gray, Sheila Levy,
and Mario Rinvolucri

Listening
Goodith White

Literature
Alan Duff and Alan Maley

Music and Song
Tim Murphey

Newspapers
Peter Grundy

Project Work 2nd edition
Diana L. Fried-Booth

Pronunciation
Clement Laroy

Role Play
Gillian Porter Ladousse

Vocabulary 2nd edition
John Morgan and Mario Rinvolucri

Writing 2nd edition
Tricia Hedge

Primary Resource Books

Art and Crafts with Children
Andrew Wright

Assessing Young Learners
Sophie Ioannou-Georgiou and
Pavlos Pavlou

Creating Stories with Children
Andrew Wright

Drama with Children
Sarah Phillips

Games for Children
Gordon Lewis with Günther Bedson

The Internet and Young Learners
Gordon Lewis

Projects with Young Learners
Diane Phillips, Sarah Burwood, and
Helen Dunford

Storytelling with Children
Andrew Wright

Very Young Learners
Vanessa Reilly and Sheila M. Ward

Writing with Children
Jackie Reilly and Vanessa Reilly

Young Learners
Sarah Phillips

Resource Books for Teachers
series editor Alan Maley

Creative Poetry Writing

Jane Spiro

OXFORD
UNIVERSITY PRESS

OXFORD
UNIVERSITY PRESS

Great Clarendon Street, Oxford OX2 6DP

Oxford University Press is a department of the University of Oxford.
It furthers the University's objective of excellence in research, scholarship,
and education by publishing worldwide in

Oxford New York

Auckland Bangkok Buenos Aires Cape Town Chennai
Dar es Salaam Delhi Hong Kong Istanbul Karachi Kolkata
Kuala Lumpur Madrid Melbourne Mexico City Mumbai Nairobi
São Paulo Shanghai Taipei Tokyo Toronto

oxford and oxford english are registered trade marks of
Oxford University Press in the UK and in certain other countries

ISBN 0 19 442189 9

Printed in China

Acknowledgements

The activities in this book were developed with language learners, teachers, poets and trainee poets in the following places and with the following classes:

Bedford College of Higher Education, UK (now de Montfort University in Bedford)
Primary Language Centres in Bedford, UK
British Council Literature workshop, Velke Mezirici, Czech Republic
Klubschule Migros, St. Gallen, Switzerland
ETAS St. Gallen, Aachen and Zurich, Switzerland
Volkshochschule Murten and Weinfelden, Switzerland
University of Nottingham Department of English Studies, Nottingham UK
British Council workshops in Pondicherry, Bangalore, Coimbatore, Chidambaram, India
British Council Cairo, Egypt
Janus Pannonius University, Pecs, Hungary
British Council Conference, Naples, Italy
British Council PRINCE project workshops in Gdansk, Torun and Vigry, Poland
Mexican B.Phil. Ed. students in Mexicali and Ensenada, Mexico
Park Primary School, Plymouth, UK
Totnes School of English, Totnes, Devon, UK
IATEFL SIG workshops: Frances King School, Bell School, International House, Westminster University, London, UK
IATEFL conferences: Edinburgh, Scotland and Dublin, Ireland
MA and BA groups, Oxford Brookes University, Oxford UK
Swedish teachers with Utbildningsstaden in Oxford, UK
International Projects Centre (IPC) Exeter
Ministry of Education Stage 3 Workshop for Literature teachers, Valbonne, France
Beijing Foreign Studies University, Beijing, China

Thanks in particular to the following projects and classes:

The first EFL poetry competition, initiated by Martin Bates, which led to the first and only EFL poetry anthology, *Poetry as a Foreign Language*.
Malaysian B.Ed groups 1993–1999 College of St. Mark and St. John, Plymouth
The Creative English class, 1998: Akiko Fukiyoshi, Kaori Hashizume, Nicholas Hirsch, Junko Hozu, Yumiko Inoue, Hiroko Kase, Miranda Loizidou, Takao Ozawa, Alice Wang, Miho Yamasaki.
The Finding Voices class at Oxford Brookes University

Thanks to students whose poems appear here and who I have not been able to trace: Eugene Larger in Mexico, Annys Blackwell in Plymouth.

Thanks to many who set up events for me to work with teachers and students: Peter Holland, Jean Rudiger, Ron Carter, Robert Bellarmine, Tracey Gilpin, Sue Parker, Liz Robbins, Lesley Hayman, Amos Paran, Gill Lazar, Cathy Pickles, Martin Bates, Cecilia Augutis, Bengt Andersson, Chrissie Mortimer, Rob Pope

Activity 1.3 first appeared as *Story as an image of life*: in *Greta* 1994, vol. 2 no. 2
Activity 10.3 first appeared as *Unlocking the Subtext* in IATEFL LitSIG newsletter, Autumn 2001.

The authors and publishers are grateful to those who have given permission to reproduce the following extracts and adaptations of copyright material:

p19 'The Loch Ness Monster's Song' by Edwin Morgan from Collected Poems by kind permission of Carcanet Press Limited.

p34 'Superman' from Collected Poems 1953–1993 by John Updike, copyright © 1993 by John Updike. Used by permission of Alfred A. Knopf, a division of Random House, Inc.

p45 'Water Everywhere' © Valerie Bloom, from Let Me Touch the Sky published by Macmillan Children's Books. Reproduced by permission.

p63 'The Love Song of J. Alfred Prufrock' from Collected Poems 1909–1962 by T. S. Eliot published by Faber and Faber Limited. Reproduced by permission of Faber and Faber Limited.

p76 'I wonder' by Opal Palmer Adisa from Nichols Grace ed. (1996) Can I buy a slice of sky?, Hodder Children's Books. Reproduced by permission of Opal Palmer Adisa.

p77 'Another filling' from Hero and the Girl Next Door by Sophie Hannah by permission of Carcanet Press Limited.

p82 'The Uncertainty of the Poet' by Wendy Cope from Poems on the Underground, Cassell 1992. Reprinted by permission of PFD on behalf of Wendy Cope.

p84 'Eleven Years Old', a selection from Earth Magic, written by Dionne Brand. Used by permission of Kids Can Press. Text © 1979 Dionne Brand.

p87 'Beehive' by J G Symons from Hiding in Chips by J Symons, 2001.

p94 'Not waving but drowning' by Stevie Smith from Norton Anthology of Modern Poetry (1973). Reproduced by permission of James & James Publishers, Executors of the Estate of James MacGibbon.

p98 'If love was Jazz' by Linda France, Poetry with an Edge, Bloodaxe Books, 1997. Reproduced by permission of Linda France.

p104 'To Michael Menser' by Benjamin Zephaniah, Too Black Too Strong, Bloodaxe Books, 2001. Reproduced by permission of Benjamin Zephaniah.

p106 'Fantasy of an African Boy' by James Berry from Emergency Kit, Faber and Faber, 1997. Reproduced by permission of James Berry.

p122 'Goodbye Now' by James Berry from A Caribbean Dozen, Walker Books, 1996. Reproduced by permission of James Berry.

p123 'The End of Love' from Hero and the Girl Next Door by Sophie Hannah by kind permission of Carcanet Press Limited.

p136 'The Figs and Biscuits' by David Bateman from Eating your Cake and Having It, Fatchance Press, 1997. Reproduced by permission of David Bateman.

p138 'Love' by John Daniel from Poetry Introduction 1, Faber and Faber. Reproduced by permission of John Daniel.

p149 'Fear and Influence' from Forgeries by James Turner, Original Plus Publication, 2002. Reproduced by permission of James Turner.

p158 'The Alphabet' by Eduardo Gonzalez Chillon from Poetry as a Foreign Language edited by Martin Bates, White Adder Press, 1999. Reproduced by permission of Martin Bates.

p165 'Autobiographia Literaria' from Collected Poems by Frank O'Hara, copyright © 1971 by Maureen Granville-Smith, Administratrix of the Estate of Frank O'Hara. Used by permission of Alfred A. Knopf, a division of Random House, Inc.

p169 'The Mother' by Anne Stevenson, The Collected Poems 1955–1995, Bloodaxe Books, 2000. Reproduced by permission of Bloodaxe Books.

p180 Haiku by Keith Harrison. Reproduced by permission of Keith Harrison.

Although every effort has been made to trace and contact copyright holders before publication, this has not been possible in some cases. We apologize for any apparent infringement of copyright and if notified, the publisher will be pleased to rectify any errors or omissions at the earliest opportunity.

Contents

Thanks to the many poet-friends who have helped to make poetry part of the patina of life; in particular John Daniel, my husband, and Charlie and Jill Hadfield, who all helped to bring this book to life.

The author and series editor

Jane Spiro is Senior Lecturer at Oxford Brookes University, and course manager of the MA in ELT for in-service teachers. She has taught language learners and teachers from beginners to MA level in schools and colleges worldwide, including Belgium, Switzerland, Hungary, Poland, India, Mexico and China. At the University of Nottingham she developed a literature testwriting programme published by Macmillan in *Assessment in Literature Teaching* (1991), in 1998 she was judge for the first Poetry in EFL competition, and consultant for the first EFL poetry anthology, *Poetry as a Foreign Language* (White Adder Press 1999).

She has written workbooks and tests, stories for language learners (*The Place of the Lotus* and *The Twin Chariot*, Thomas Nelson, *Travelling light* in *London Tales* with ELI Naples), and has written and presented six programmes on cross-cultural issues for Carlton television. She has also had poetry published in the US and UK and been shortlisted for several poetry prizes. In 2002 she published her first novel, *Nothing I Touch Stands Still* (Crucible Press).

Alan Maley worked for The British Council from 1962 to 1988, serving as English Language Officer in Yugoslavia, Ghana, Italy, France, and China, and as Regional Representative in South India (Madras). From 1988 to 1993 he was Director-General of the Bell Educational Trust, Cambridge. From 1993 to 1998 he was Senior Fellow in the Department of English Language and Literature of the National University of Singapore, and from 1998 to 2003 he was Director of the graduate programme at Assumption University, Bangkok. He is currently a freelance consultant. Among his publications are *Literature* (in this series), *Beyond Words*, *Sounds Interesting*, *Sounds Intriguing*, *Words*, *Variations on a Theme*, and *Drama Techniques in Language Learning* (all with Alan Duff), *The Mind's Eye* (with Françoise Grellet and Alan Duff), *Learning to Listen* and *Poem into Poem* (with Sandra Moulding), *Short and Sweet*, and *The English Teacher's Voice*.

Foreword

Until recently, language teaching methodology had little time for the more creative and playful uses of language. The structural approaches tended to focus on the form of the language, and the communicative approaches on the pragmatic, utilitarian aspects of language use. Slowly, however, the realization has begun to dawn that language is more than just day-to-day 'communication'. A great deal of language use is actually playful, with no immediate communicative pay-off. One has only to think of the frequency of language play in the domains of advertising and newspaper headlines. And children acquire their first language in part by playing with its rhymes and rhythms, with scant attention to communicative value.

This book is an important contribution to redressing the balance between 'referential' and 'representational' uses of language. It demonstrates how language can be introduced in a pleasurable context, so that repetition and focus on form are an integral part of the process. It further shows how memorable highly patterned, playful language can be.

Nonetheless, some people find the idea of writing poetry, especially in a foreign language, somewhat intimidating. Others might object that 'creative' writing is a waste of time because it appears to be unfocused and undisciplined. This book amply demonstrates that neither of these misgivings is justified. There is a progression in the activities from sounds, through words and sentences, to more complex work on genres, games, and stories. The activities offer students a structured and non-threatening approach to using language creatively, and yet with also the communicative purpose of bringing their personal experience to bear. Furthermore, the language teaching and learning is an integral part of this process. It is by no means neglected.

This is a cornucopia of ingenious yet simple and practical ideas. Teachers will find it easy to use. Students will find it a delight.

Alan Maley

Introduction

Why was this book written?

The first poems many children hear are the words of favourite songs, the jingles of advertisements, nursery rhymes and the spells of wizards in fairy tales. These were my first encounters with poetry too, and they left the clear impression that rhyme was magic. It conjured stories; it created the frisson of surprise and yet order; it bound you into a cabal of secret meanings. This sense of its magic did not diminish with growing up. On the contrary, poetry revealed its capacity not only to open other worlds, but also to explain and illuminate this one.

This view seemed to sit uncomfortably with an increasingly functional view of language. Our era is one in which the business-driven world of corporate meanings and conventional formulae is more valued than the life of the imagination. We work hard to teach the language that will help our learners interact with the real world; but are we leaving them and ourselves behind in doing so?

This book was written because it became clear to me that the messages generated by the communicative classroom were worthy, but simply weren't enough. The learner had more to communicate, and the structures we were teaching had more messages to yield than we had yet explored. When language learners are invited to speak more fully, they can be funny, wise, child-like, playful, witty, sentimental, philosophical, experimental. They can be many things there is no room to be in the functional classroom. The progress made by humanistic and communicative teaching and by the different pedagogic approaches to language can combine to take us further as learners and teachers.

Who is this book for?

This book is for teachers who would like to give their learners the opportunity to say and do more with the language they are practising. It is for teachers who wish to add a sense of production, excitement, and performance to the language classroom, to give students the opportunity to say something surprising and original, even while they practise new aspects of language.

With few exceptions, the activities can be set up with no resources at all, apart from a blackboard, and paper for the students to write on. However, resources such as pictures, wall posters, and home-made recordings of poems will supplement the activities well if teachers have these facilities. Nor do the activities require special slots in the timetable designated 'creative writing'. They can be integrated into the coursebook and can support the language syllabus, whether it is functional, notional, situational, grammatical, humanistic, all of these or none of these.

The activities draw on 20 years' experience in language classrooms involving all levels, ages, backgrounds, and purposes. Some of the poems cited here are composite poems generated by a whole class, or by several groups over a number of years; their lines and ideas were recorded in notebooks, diaries, and lesson plans. These classes have been eclectic, to say the least. They include primary language centres in Bedford in the early 1980s, Turkish Cypriot children in a Haringey primary school, Vietnamese asylum-seekers in Bedford, Malaysian B.Ed. students in Plymouth, Swiss adult language learners, Hungarian doctors in ESP classes, multicultural adult language groups, teacher and student groups in and from Belgium, Hungary, Poland, France, Sweden, Sri Lanka, India, China, Japan, and Mexico.

What does this book try to do?

This book gives teachers practical ideas for teaching language through poetry. Every activity is introduced with clear aims that connect with the language syllabus. You are provided with language examples to help develop activities and support your students. The activities can be used as a course, starting with sounds, and moving on to words, phrases, sentences and whole texts. Or they can be used in any order, as separate self-contained activities.

In each activity, learners will write a poem which can be included in a class anthology, displayed on the walls, performed in class. There is a praise-song they can dance to, a poetry market they can set up in class, a theatre of inner and outer voices they can perform chorally. Or they can simply write quietly, in pairs, groups, or individually. The lessons show that even beginners can do interesting things with language: they can join words, sounds, and rhythms together, experiment with the shape and form of words on the page, build and break down the parts of words. For more advanced learners, there are accessible and memorable lessons which look at sentences, idioms, and metaphors; focus on cultural information in words and ways of telling stories, describing family and friends, memories, values, and dreams, and so on.

The activities are very easy to use. Each one is introduced with a short warm-up. There are also suggestions for how teachers might correct student work after the task, and which aspects of accuracy can be focused on. Some teachers may find individual students who cannot respond to a task, or specific tasks which just don't match the class. Some activities offer a set of alternatives and suggestions about large classes, mixed ability groups, shy students, or the special interests of boys or girls. These classroom tips make it possible to tailor these activities to your own class, and what you know will work for your students.

No special materials are needed. All teachers need is a blackboard. Nor do teachers need any specialist knowledge. The technical words are explained in a glossary at the end of the book, and you are guided towards these within the activity. There are also further publications listed in the appendix for teachers who would like to go further with their classes.

The lessons aim to show teachers both what is familiar and what is special about poetry, and how poetry can be a rich resource in learning a language.

Why poetry?

Poetry is peculiarly suited to the demands of the language classroom. It is inevitable that a focus on form is not what we really do when we give messages in the everyday world. But interestingly, it is, or can be, what we do when we write poetry. In fact, for some a focus on form and language is exactly what makes poetry different from other written texts. Interestingly, controlled language practice has several features typical of poetry: repetition, pattern, and length. The less controlled stages of language practice encourage the learner to be creative and to use strategies for applying the familiar to the unfamiliar – just as poets do.

The quality of repetition

A feature of poetic form is repetition of a single word, line, or group of lines. The villanelle repeats its opening line and third line at varied intervals in a 19-line sequence; the sestina repeats six end-words; the ballad has a refrain of several lines between each stanza. A well-known example of the villanelle is Dylan Thomas's *Do not go gentle into that good night*. This line, memorable as it is, becomes more so when repeated like an echo through six stanzas. The repetition acquires a new resonance each time it occurs, carrying with it the sense of all the previous lines. From a mechanical point of view, a language drill repeats in the same way:

Is Alice thirsty?
Is Alice hungry?
Is Alice tired?

The structure might, like a refrain, repeat itself through the entire discourse of a language lesson.

The quality of pattern

The poet will deliberately draw attention to patterns of sound, of spelling, of structure. Rhyme is an orally/aurally apparent example of sound patterns, as are alliteration and assonance. But the poet may also, like the language teacher, draw attention to structure deliberately. Here are lines from a poem by Benjamin Zephaniah which use the pattern *I want/I don't want*:

> I want babies that will live for a lifetime,
> I don't want to silence their souls
> I don't want them to be seen and not heard,
> I want them to be heard
> I want them loud and proud.

Of course, both the examples above illustrate an important difference between poetry and the language drill – the emotional content.

> Do not go gentle into that good night
> Rage, rage against the dying of the light

These are not lines that merely repeat: they convey an accumulating power, carrying with each repetition the sense of the preceding stanza – old age, the wise, the good, the wild, even 'my father' must all face 'the dying of the light'. Similarly, in the Zephaniah poem, the structures are not repeated for the sake of the verb form, but to describe a vision of the future.

So here we have a perfect model for the language classroom. On the one hand, there is a focus on language. On the other, permission to reveal the inner story. Another way learners may look at it is that they are practising the language being taught whilst communicating something they actually want to say. The first becomes the vehicle for the second.

The length of poems

Another aspect of poems which makes them particularly useful in the classroom is that they are usually short. But is this important and why?

A shorter text means there are fewer words to convey your message, so every word is important. Because every word is important, poets use many techniques to give their language power. For example, repeating vowel and consonant sounds to create patterns of sound, making words rhyme to create 'music' through words, creating pictures, puns, surprising contrasts and juxtapositions of ideas.

Poets make language a surprise, and they make it memorable in the way a song or a jingle can be memorable.

A poem can tell us about a single thought or episode, a single image or moment in time. There is no subject too small for a poem. Some of the best poems are about very, very small things: a red wheelbarrow, a plate of plums, a horse rubbing its back against a tree, a flea crawling across a table.

On the other hand, no subject is too big for a poem. Homesickness, alienation, disappointment, insecurity, excitement, opportunity, tenderness are not subjects we can usually talk about in a language lesson, but we can talk about them in a poem.

When we write well, we make people listen to us, feel as we do, step into our shoes.

The use of learner strategies

Learners experiment with unfamiliar language in just the way that poets do. For example:

- learners take a language 'rule' and apply it in new places, to create an 'invented' word which expresses their meaning. Searching for two + ten, a learner creates the word '*Twenteen*' (Gavin Bantock in *Poetry as a Foreign Language*).
- learners search for a vocabulary item they need, and if they do not know it, replace it with a synonym or a newly constructed word. A learner, searching for the word *brother-in-law*, creates my *sister-husband*, or searching for the word *jeep,* creates the word *adventure car*.
- learners transfer the sounds, rhythms, and patterns of their mother tongue into the foreign language. In so doing, they create 'new' words and patterns which belong half in one, and half in another culture. In the same way, poets treat language as if they are meeting it for the first time, as if it is strange, unfamiliar and new. This strangeness is part of what learners experience all the time – they can look at language with the same distance and freshness as the poet aims to do.

What about the errors learners make?

Some teachers who use these activities may be concerned that their learners might make mistakes or try and use language they haven't yet learnt. There are several points to make here.

Each activity has a particular language aim, which is carefully modelled for the less advanced student. If teachers are concerned with accuracy, accuracy in this specific area could be encouraged. But we recommend that other inaccuracies be overlooked, and are recognized as part of the creative process – creative in that the learners are seeking strategies for filling gaps in their knowledge. Some of these strategies may in themselves involve an imaginative leap such as those in the examples above. Cultivating these strategies is an important part of the learning process, and can be used in another lesson as springboards for learning.

Over-concern about errors can be an inhibiting factor for the learner. One of the frustrations for adults learning a language is that their cognitive abilities are often so much in advance of their vocabulary that they are forced to reduce their messages in terms of complexity, depth and knowledge of the world. The activities in this book encourage even the elementary learner to find vehicles for these more complex thoughts, and offer frameworks and support so the learner can also be accurate in specific areas modelled by the task.

Can creative writing help students to write well?

When students write about themselves, there is a reason for writing. This is not an activity with an answer key, or one which can be done equally well by a friend or by a teacher. Only the student knows what they really want to say. There is a reason, then, for making the poem as 'good' as possible: it may be performed, it may be displayed on the wall or put in a class anthology. Writing a poem includes exchanging ideas, writing, then editing, asking friends to read and respond, and rewriting. It gives real and meaningful practice in all the skills of writing.

Can creative writing help students to read well?

When students write more confidently, they read more confidently too. The writing activities in this book develop an appreciation of the sounds and rhythms of language, sentence patterns, the shape and meaning of words, how words and sentences connect with one another to form texts, and the features of different text types. All of these are the skills of the confident reader too. By understanding better what it feels like to be a writer, students will also be more active and confident in their enjoyment of reading.

What do poems have to do with everyday language?

Some people may say that poetry is not typical of the language students will need to use. But everyday language uses many devices traditionally thought of as 'poetic'. In fact to recognize and use these is part of our skill as language users.

We use metaphors and similes every day, just like poets. *To see red* means *to be angry*. But why is anger red? *To headhunt* means to choose the best person for a job – but is it really about hunting heads? *To count one's chickens* means to have unrealistic expectations. But why?!

Just like poets, we create 'new' words by changing their function: *parent*, for example, is used as a verb in our generation – *to parent*. This shows us that being a parent is something active. It isn't just something you ARE, but something you DO as well.

Businesses try to sell us products by using 'catchy' phrases and names that rhyme, or repeating sounds like the /k/ sound in *Coca-Cola*, or playing with the meaning of words.

This is just what poets do – they 'invent' language in order to explain more exactly their message, and they bring words together so that they surprise or suggest.

Far from being removed from everyday life, 'poetic language' is more and more part of modern English. It is the way we make people, places and products, feelings and experiences memorable. To recognize this is to appreciate the colourfulness of everyday speech.

Do students have to follow rules when they write poems?

Yes and no. The interesting thing about poems is that the poet can choose.

For example, a poet can decide to write a poem without any verbs at all, or to write a poem which only uses names. They can decide to write a poem in groups of three lines, or four lines, or in one long paragraph, or even make their poem create a shape on the page. The poem does whatever the poet wants it to do. It is the poet's way of telling us – 'This is what I want to say.'

For more proficient learners, the language in poetry is an excellent starting point for discussion. How does a different choice of word change the meaning? How many meanings does one line have? What if the pronoun was different? Or the tense?

The exciting thing about poems is that the poet is the one who makes up the rules.

What can we do with poems once they are written?

A poem is different from a letter, memo, or other classroom writing task. A poem can be sung, chanted chorally, orchestrated, accompanied by drums and pipes, dance and mime. It can be turned into a class anthology; it can be collected in a personal anthology; it can feed into diaries and biographies, photograph albums, posters, wall displays, and love letters. As soon as your learners' poems are 'published' in this way, their thoughts take on a life of their own. Other learners can read, interpret, and be inspired by them.

My learners don't like using their imagination. Will they enjoy writing poems?

Some teachers are concerned that their learners 'don't like using their imaginations'. Maybe, for example, adult learners will find certain imaginative leaps childish, not useful, and not relevant to the learning process. All of these are valid responses, and it is certainly true that some of these activities do involve journeys into fantasy and imagination. However, most work with 'everyday' life, thoughts, beliefs, hopes, relationships, and the only leap your learners will need is the realization that familiar language patterns can indeed express all these things.

However adult learners sometimes enjoy the 'imaginative' activities more than we might expect. It may be over-protective of us as teachers to assume that they will not. It must be left to each teacher and each class to assess the likely response here, but some surprises I have had in developing these activities include:

- a group of rather hostile teenagers who chose to write extremely gentle rhyming love poems, and were entirely absorbed in the creation of them (in Activity 1.4)
- a group of grammar-oriented adults who became hugely amused and involved in the 'poetry market' (Activity 6.5)
- a group of shy and insecure adult learners who created a powerful 'sound poem' for the rest of the class, clearly recounting the story of their civil war (Activity 1.2)
- a worried First Certificate class which had not really bonded, joining together to write a riotous praise-song to their examiner (Activity 7.6).

Learner reactions to these activities have been so diverse and unpredictable that I have learnt to expect nothing.

How to use this book

How is the book organized?

The book starts with the smallest unit of language – individual sounds.

Each chapter moves on to bigger 'chunks' of language – parts of words (syllables, morphemes, suffixes, and prefixes), whole words and their rhythm, sentences and how they express time and meaning, sentence patterns and shapes, the way sentences are joined together, texts and text types.

Teachers can 'dip' into any of these chapters to supplement the language lesson, whether it be a revision task for the present perfect, or an activity to develop free writing skills in the proficiency class.

Within each unit, the learners will:

1 practise an aspect of language of value to the learning process, such as word-building skills, idioms, pronunciation and spelling links, forming statements, questions and negative forms
2 apply the language point to experiences, memories, and feelings of their own, through carefully guided activities
3 compare their own products with those of other students and of published writers, if appropriate and desired
4 be led towards a 'product' which can be shared with others in the class, such as a poem, a poster, or a performance.

The activities are grouped together, according to which language point they practise.

Chapter 1:   the sounds of English
Chapter 2:   the building blocks of words, such as prefixes, suffixes, and grammatical changes in words
Chapter 3:   how words connect into idioms, collocations, and what happens when words are mixed and compared
Chapter 4:   how sentences are formed
Chapter 5:   how we express time through tense and aspect in verbs
Chapter 6:   how we express meaning through modal forms
Chapter 7:   the phrases and formulae we use in different everyday situations
Chapter 8:   how texts are adapted to match their purpose and audience
Chapter 9:   poems as visual objects and as group games
Chapter 10: poems as moments in a story

Within each chapter, some activities will be for complete beginners, encouraging them to play with the sounds of English, but others will be for advanced learners, encouraging them to examine their own assumptions, expand their understanding of words and meanings. Many of the activities can be adapted to any level, as they offer you the chance to adapt, change, and add to the language examples given.

Most of the warm-up stages include building a short 'class poem' on the blackboard.

There are several ways these poems could be read aloud:

- the whole class reads together, as a chorus
- each line is read by a different learner or group of learners
- the lines are read alternately, with the class divided into two halves, so one half seems to answer the other
- teachers read a line, with the class 'answering' with the second line
- the lines are read so they 'overlap' one another and form a kind of 'cascade' of sound. This works when one learner or group reads a line and the second line is started before the first has finished, and so on.

In each activity, there are one or more poems which may help you, or offer an example to your students. You could use these activity poems in many different ways:

- Write them on posters and place them round the walls of your classroom as an inspiration while the students work.
- Write them on the blackboard while the students are writing their own poems, and compare the two versions at the end of the lesson.
- Copy the poems on to a worksheet, and distribute them to students to read for homework before the lesson, or after the lesson.
- Read the poem aloud to the students at the beginning of the lesson as an inspiration, then let them read a written version at the end, when they have created their own poems.

Routes through the activities

You could 'travel' through the book in several different ways.

1 Select activities according to topics you are covering in class. Topics are listed in the index, and you could choose activities that cluster around different themes, such as the family, gifts, friends, monuments, dreams and hopes, childhood memories, birthdays, etc.
2 Select activities according to structures or functions you are teaching. Again, these are listed in the index and in the contents page for quick reference and include functions such as asking directions, praising, complaining, and grammatical elements such as modals, question forms, complex sentences, tenses and verb patterns, phrases and sentence structure.

3 Select activities at random simply to warm up or close down a lesson, change the group dynamic, or introduce a surprise and change to the usual pattern.

4 Set up a project and use the activities as a route towards this goal. For example, producing a class anthology, or preparing a short performance of sketches, songs, and readings for other classes.

For further ideas and information about poetry and using this book, visit our website http://www.oup.com/elt/teacher/rbt which includes downloadable worksheets, extra activities, links, articles, interviews, and competitions for students.

1 Sound poems

This chapter looks at the combinations of sounds which make words in the English language. The activities give students who have just started the language the chance to express ideas through sounds alone. They also give them a sense of which combinations are possible in English, and how they differ from the mother tongue. There are also activities which will be interesting and challenging for advanced students: exploring their interpretation of words and sounds, and where these come from in their background knowledge. Some activities encourage students to make links between the sounds and spellings of words, and, where these exist, between sound and meaning. Other activities look at what sounds mean in different cultures and languages: for example, how different cultures express surprise or interest, or the way animal noises are expressed. There is an emphasis on experimentation, so that the language is fun and elements of the word can be played with like plasticine, to give students confidence and courage. There is also an emphasis, for the more advanced learner, on exploring what they already know, testing their assumptions about language, and exploring the source of these assumptions.

1.1 Animal sound poems: *Contented lions*

Level Elementary to advanced

Time 25 minutes

Aims To enable students to explore the kind of sounds and sound clusters which appear in English words.

To encourage students to experiment with language and create these patterns for themselves.

Materials
- The picture at the top of the next page.
- Sound lists 1 and 2 written on the board or on a roll of paper.
- The **Loch Ness monster poem**.

Preparation

1 Before the lesson begins, write Sound lists 1 and 2 on to the blackboard, an OHT, or a large roll of paper, which you should pin to the wall for use during the lesson.

These are groups of sounds which are often found in English words. Each letter in these clusters is sounded. There are no silent letters in this list.

Sound list 1 Sounds beginning words	Sound list 2 Sounds ending words
dr	mp
gr	nk
br	rk
st	st
sp	nd
cr	nt
bl	sk
cl	sp
fl	
gl	
pr	
pl	
shr	
sl	
tr	

2   Practise **The Loch Ness monster** poem below, either so you can read it yourself in the lesson, or record it on tape so that you can play it in class. There is no correct way to read it, so enjoy the strange sounds and combinations.

> **The Loch Ness monster**
>
> Ssnnwhuffflll?
> Hnwhuffl hhnwfl hnfl hfl?
> Gdrlblboblhobngbl gbl gl g g g g glbgl.
> Drublhaflablhaflubhafgabhaflhafl fl fl –
> gm grawwww grf grawf awfgm graw gm,
> Hovplodok – doplodovok – plovodokot – doplodokosh?
> Splgraw fok fok splgrafhatchgabrlgabrl fok splfok!
> Zgra kra gka fok!
> Grof grawff gahf?
> Gombl mbl bl –
> blm plm,
> blm plm,
> blm plm,
> blp.
>
> *Edwin Morgan*

3   Check **consonant clusters** in the glossary.

Procedure

1   Show your students the pictures at the beginning of this activity.
What does each animal feel? How do we know?

What noises do other animals make?
What noises do YOU make when you feel surprised? sad? angry?

Invite your students to suggest some emotions and some animal noises.

How would you write these noises?

Invite them to look through the list of word beginnings and endings, and see if they can 'write down' some of these sounds.

2   If you feel able and confident to read the Loch Ness monster poem aloud to your students, this is an exciting way to start the lesson.

Ask them to listen to the poem. *What could it be? A person, animal, type of weather? A place or a feeling?*

Give your class the chance to guess, then write the title of the poem on the blackboard: **The Loch Ness monster**.

3   Ask the students to give you the names of three animals or insects, either in English or in the mother tongue. Write these up on the blackboard, with an English translation where necessary/possible.

snake	bee	lion

4 Now suggest your class experiment with the sounds in Sound list 1 above, individually or in groups, and choose one sound which suits each animal.

They can practise stretching out each sound in the pair *sssssssslllllllllllll* or repeating the sound *drdrdrdrdr*.

5 When the class have had time experimenting, write up the choices on the blackboard, inviting the class to help you with the spelling of each noise.

Your blackboard may now look something like this:

Group A	Group B	Group C
snake	bee	lion
sssssssssslllllllllllllll	drdrdrdrdr	prrrr prrrr prrrr
sssssssshhhhhh		grrrrrrr grrrrrr

6 Use all the examples in each list as class poems. Invite the class to perform these by reading them aloud.

7 Ask students now to look at the sounds in Sound list 2 above. Invite them to experiment by attaching the word ends to the word beginnings, using any combinations that they like. They can say these aloud to themselves or in small groups, mixing and matching. For example, *slmp drnk blmp plnk grnd.*

8 When they have had time experimenting, invite students to invent words to describe how each animal moves or eats.

Elicit some of their ideas, and write these up on the board.

snake
shhhhhhllllllll
slmp slmp slmp

9 Now students can work in small groups, to choose their own animals, and invent their own sounds for the animal and the way it moves or eats perhaps adding other sound effects as in the poem about the cat in the snow on the following page.

10 After ten minutes, invite each group to prepare a 'performance' of their poem. The others in the class should listen, and guess the animal.

You may also want to share the following poem written by Swiss students.

Cat in the Snow

brrrr brrrrr

plp plp plp

brrrr brrrr

plplplplplp
shwashwashwahswahswa
shwashwashwashwa
shwashwashwashwah

miaoooouww miaoooouww
brrrrrrrr brrrrrrrrrr

plp

Swiss language teachers, Murten

Variations

The following topics have also worked well as sound poems:

computer
mobile phone
train
aeroplane
river
storm
seasons: autumn, spring, summer, winter
school bell

Each group could choose a topic, and make sound poems as a riddle for other students to guess.

Comments

This activity can work with students who are meeting English for the first time. It is designed to give them confidence with the combinations of sounds typical in English.

However, this activity has also been tried out with advanced students with much success and enjoyment. For advanced students it could be a way of sensitizing them to sounds and sound clusters, which are the building blocks of words.

1.2 Onomatopoeic poems: *Snoring Englishmen*

Level Elementary to upper-intermediate

Time 25 minutes

Aims To focus on the noises we make to express feelings and to practise ways in which these noises and sounds vary in different languages and cultures.

Materials

- The picture at the beginning of this activity.
- The list of noises.
- A reading of **The Blacksmiths**.

Preparation

1 Before you start the lesson, you may want to draw up a list of which noises and sounds are used in your students' mother tongue in particular situations. A list drawn up for English might look something like this:

Sound	When?
ow! ouch! /aʊ/	you sit on a pin
oy! hey! /ɔɪ/	you want to catch someone's attention
mm mm	you want to show you are listening to someone
oh!	you are surprised
phew!	you are relieved about something
plop	falling water
crash	cars colliding
smash	knocking someone out, hitting someone
clunk	the sound of metal against metal, something heavy falling

2 Practise *The Blacksmiths* so you can read it yourself in the lesson, or record it on tape so that you can play it in class. In Middle English, each letter would probably have been sounded, but there is no correct version of the reading, so enjoy the strange sounds and words.

This poem was written by an anonymous poet some time between 1425–1450. At that time the English language combined features of Anglo-Saxon and Norman French. This is why it looks different from modern English.

The Blacksmiths

What knavene cry and clateryng of knockes!
The cammede kongons cryen after 'col! col!'
And blow their bellows, that all here brayn brestes:
"Huf, puf!" says one, "haf, paf!" that other.
They spitten and spraulen and spellyn many spelles:
They gnawen and gnashen, they groan together
Lus, bus! las, das!
Tik, tak! hic, hac! tiket, taket! tyk, tak
Lus, bys! lus, das!
extract from a 14th-century alliterative poem: anonymous

3 Check **onomatopoeia** in the glossary.

Procedure

1 Invite students to look at the picture at the beginning of this activity. What do the sounds tell us about each character? Ask students to compare noises they make in different situations, for example, sitting on a pin. The ideas you prepared before the class may help you. If students need more help ask them what sound we would use:

- *to show we are listening carefully?*
- *to show we are surprised?*
- *to show a character is sleeping?*

If you heard only the sounds alone, would you be able to guess what was happening?

2 Read *The Blacksmiths* without giving the title of the poem. Ask students to tell you what they imagine as they listen. *Is it people, animals or landscape? Is it water, land, or air? If it is people, what are they doing? Are they happy, tired, busy, angry? What title would you give the poem?*

Here are some ideas:
people working hard, sweating and straining at their work; people rushing to work

Discussion questions for more advanced students:

- *Why did you think the poem was about … ?*
- *Were there particular sounds which helped you make that decision?*
- *What noises do you make when you sit on a pin, when you are very tired, when you want to attract attention?*
- *What noises do you think an English-speaking person would make in each of these situations?*

3 Ask students to add a second verse to the poem, based on their interpretations of the first verse. They can use words and sounds of their own to continue with their idea of what it is about.

4 When they have finished, ask students to prepare a 'performance' of their second verse in groups of two or three. The noises could be repeated, or sounded out by three people at once, or they could overlap and interrupt each other. The 'poet' can decide.
Ask students to perform their poem to others in the class.
While they listen, it is the task of the class to guess or to suggest a title for the poem.

Variations

If your class has enjoyed this activity and would like to make more sound poems, you could ask them to choose one from the list below.

- *a baby being fed*
- *running to catch a train or a bus*
- *a climber climbing a mountain*
- *typists in a typing pool*
- *someone doing the laundry*
- *trying to get rid of a wasp or mosquito*

Comments

The main question to ask is:

Do the sounds suggest the feelings that are intended?

The students can give one another feedback about this.

Otherwise, there is no right or wrong in this activity. Its aim is to enjoy the sounds, and notice what feelings and moods they suggest.

1.3 Nickname poems: *Garihumbabi, pyramid priest*

Level Elementary to intermediate

Time 25 minutes

Aims To investigate the sound and meaning of nicknames and to practise adjectives for describing people.

Procedure

1 Ask the students to think about nicknames they have used in childhood or adulthood. Nicknames could include those given to favourite or least favourite schoolteachers, siblings and members of the family, toys, and pets. Write up their examples on the board.
If your class are not sure what *nickname* means, offer some nicknames of your own or of other people as an example. For example: *Zunzun is the noise my son made whenever he heard his father's car drive up: so we call him Zunzun now.*

These are some names which have been gathered from students on workshops in Hungary, India, and Britain. They may be useful as a starting point if your own students do not have suggestions of their own.

Sample nicknames

Garihumbabi	*Buba*
Mimi	*Woolly*
Baldylocks	*Minka*
Zsomle	*Faez*
Toto	*Zunzun*

2   Choose two or three names from the examples which look particularly interesting. Ask the person who gave the example to stay quiet while the class talks about the name. See if the class can suggest:

- if the name belongs to a person, toy, or pet
- if a person, whether this is male or female
- what kind of person, toy, or pet: what information can they guess about the owner of the name?

3   Elicit some examples of their ideas, and write these on the board. For example:

Garihumbabi, priest of the Egyptian pyramids
Buba, round and cuddly Russian grandma
Minka, the silky black Persian cat

When the group have shared their ideas, see if the person who suggested the name can give the 'real' information. The names, with their description, are the first few lines of a class poem.

4   Now ask students to work in groups of two and three.

Each group should choose one name which they are not familiar with. They should then write as many words as they can to describe the owner of the name. They can use a dictionary to help, or the following list of words may help them.

Adjectives describing people and pets

bouncy	*round*
curly-haired	*plump*
silky	*proud*
cuddly	*furry*
naughty	*bald*
greedy	*hairy*

Here is an example:

> Toto
> small furry bouncy
> brown curly funny
> greedy naughty
> dog

5   When the class is ready, ask each group to read back their verse, moving from one nickname to the next around the class.

1.4 Rhyming poems: *Heart where you feel*

Level Lower-intermediate to advanced

Time 25 minutes

Aims To experiment with words that have the same vowel sounds and to experiment with rhyme and assonance.

Preparation

1 Choose two or three of the columns below. On the blackboard, write **two or three** of the words from each column which your students already know.

You could choose words of your own which form rhyming patterns, and which you know your students understand.

All the words in each column share the same vowel sound. This sound is shown by the phonetic symbol at the top of the list.

/eɪ/	/ɑː/	/ɔː/	/iː/	/æ/
pale	heart	tall	wheel	cat
fail	art	Paul	feel	hat
sail	part	shawl	meal	fat
male	tart	small	deal	rat
rail	start	wall	heel	mat
tail	cart	ball	seal	chat
whale	dart	call	real	flat
nail	smart	fall		

2 Check **rhyme words** and **assonance** in the glossary.

Procedure

1 Ask students to look at the rhyming words you have put in each column on the blackboard. Ask them if they notice what the words in each column have in common. Encourage them to notice all the words have the same vowel sound AND the same last consonant sound. These are all rhymes.

2 Divide the class into groups of three or four, and give each group two minutes to think of as many words as they can which belong in each of the columns.

3 Ask groups to share their words with you, and write these up in the columns on the board. Ask the class how many spellings they notice in each column for the same vowel sound.

4 Now ask the class to work again in small groups. Each group must choose **one** column of rhyme words. Ask them to choose three of the rhyming words which they like or which seem to connect in some way. For each rhyme word, they must write a short explanation – a phrase or short sentence.

Here are examples from other students:

> heart when you feel
> part when I hurt
> dart bull's eye hit
>
> when you feel   heart
> when I hurt   part
> bull's eye hit   dart

Teachers at a Valentine's Day workshop, London

> round and brown cat
> fat and furry cat
> cat finds mouse
> squashes it flat

Children in Plymouth, Poets in School workshop

If there are any more words in the column, they should continue in the same way, writing the word and then its definition, in groups of three words.

5 For students that work fast, or run out of words, ask them to choose another rhyme pattern: either one of the columns on the board or another rhyme pattern of their own. They should then continue in the same way, writing 'verses' of word + short definition. They can write these in 'verses' of three lines or four lines.

6 After ten minutes, ask students to read their verses aloud to one another in small groups or to the whole class.

Comments

Check that the spelling of the vowel sound is correct in each word. Encourage the students to use dictionaries to check their own spelling. An important part of this lesson is to show the different ways the same sound can be spelt.

1.5 Rhythm poems: *Gone to London*

Level Elementary to intermediate

Time 25 minutes

Aims To help the whole class recognize and enjoy the rhythm in words and groups of words and to practise the pronunciation of proper nouns.

Preparation

Check **proper nouns** in the glossary.

Procedure

1 Tell your students they are going to write and perform story poems using names of people and places only. For this they will need only a paper and pen.

They must listen to your question, and write down the name of a person or place only for each answer.

Verse 1
Write down:
Your name
The name of a best friend
The place you last saw your best friend

Verse 2
Write down:
Your name
Where you are now

Verse 3
Write down:
Your friend's name
Where your friend is now

If your students are unlikely to have friends in distant places, or if it is likely all their answers will be similar, change and adapt the questions to offer more varied answers. But the rule must stay the same: answers should be NAMES only!

2   Encourage students to experiment by rearranging and repeating the names in different ways to tell a story. Pauses – shown by gaps between lines – might be part of the story. Putting words close together and saying them quickly without pauses might also help to tell the story. In this way, they can use rhythms to add extra meaning to their stories.
They can also experiment with different voices for performing their poem aloud: a female 'chorus' or voice for the female names, a male 'chorus' for the male names, for example.

Here is a poem produced at a teachers' workshop in Budapest. Can you guess the story?

> Margit Margit
> Zoltan Zoltan
>
> Margit Budapest Zoltan
> Zoltan Budapest Margit
>
> Margit London
> Zoltan Budapest
>
> Zoltan Margit Budapest
> Zoltan Margit London
>
> Margit London
> Zoltan Budapest
>
> Zoltan
>
> Margit
>
> *Workshop with Hungarian teachers, Budapest*

Variations

A variation of this activity is to use the names with different intonation, to tell a story.

So, for example:

Junko?
Junko??
Junko!!

Comments

The only language point to check is that all the names are written with capital letters. Encourage your students to use pauses and pace to tell their story.

1.6 Alliterative poems: *The Cute Creams*

Level Lower-intermediate to upper-intermediate

Time 25 minutes

Aims To draw attention to the opening sounds of words and the concept of alliteration.

Preparation

1 Prepare the following plan on the board, or on a roll of paper you can display in the classroom. Choose words your students will know. Add others of your own to each column.

The lists of words are in alphabetical order.

Column A lists adjectives
Column B lists food words
Column C lists animals

Column A	Column B	Column C
amazing	apple	bee
angry	butter	cat
brave	cream	dragon
cool	eggs	elephant
cute	honey	hen
dancing	milk	mouse
dangerous	orange	tiger
evil	sugar	
happy		
high		
mad		
manly (like a man)		
old		
sure		
tiny		

2 Check **alliteration** in the glossary.

Procedure

1 Show students the words on the blackboard. Ask them if they can see why the words are grouped in the way they are.

They could answer:
- *they are in alphabetical order*
- *all the words in column A are describing words/adjectives*
- *all the words in column B are food*
- *all the words in column C are animals*

Ask them to suggest other words to add to each list, and write these on the board.

2 Explain that the class has been asked by an advertising company to find an exciting name and a short advertising slogan for a new fruit drink or food product, or, for a new pop group.

The food company/pop group have asked them to choose:
- a name with two words
- each word must start with the same sound
- the slogan must describe the product very briefly, using at least one word with the same first sound.

Here are some examples, using the words in the list:

Angry Apple, amazing rock sound! (a rock band)
High Honey, heavenly, healthy! (soft drink)

Ask students to suggest examples of the names of real rock bands, fruit drinks, and food products and see if they follow the rules above. If they do, write these on the board. For example, *Coca-Cola*.

3 Ask students to work in groups of two or three and make their own names, using words on the board or words of their own. Ask each group to draw up a list of:
four pop-group names OR four food names, using the same rules (two words, each starting with the same sound).

4 Beside each name, they should write their 'slogan' – a few words explaining why the pop group or food product is special, with at least one word using the same initial sound. Here are some examples:

Cute Creams: the coolest singing kids in town!
Brave Butter Bees: best chocolate snack for busy people!
Mouse milk: mild medicine for muddled minds

5 After ten minutes, ask the groups to read the names to others in the class. The best names could be written on posters, and put on the wall to work on or illustrate in a later class.

Comments

The main language point to check is that students have chosen words with the same first sound. Sometimes the spelling in English may be confusing. For example, the first sound in the word *sugar* /ʃ/ is more frequently spelt *sh,* as in *shining, shameless. Sugar* does not have the same first sound as *sucks*, despite the spelling being similar. Check your students' pairs of words, and make sure the words sound the same. In the examples above, words have been chosen where the sound and the spelling are the same.

2
Wordplay poems

The first three activities in this chapter explore the building blocks of words: prefixes, suffixes, and morphemes. The activities show how parts of words are detachable, and how, when they are joined to new words, they are able to change their meaning and function. The activities explore how a whole family of words can be built from just one root, using these building blocks. Students will practise building their own words as well as unpacking words they already know and making them open up into different meanings.

The second three activities explore the meanings embedded in words. The activities invite students to think about where meaning comes from: whether from cultural information, knowledge of the world, associations with other sounds and words in their language, from myths and stories, or from personal experience. It invites students to use understanding of words as a way of expressing their understanding of the world.

Although the emphasis is on play and experimentation, the activities are designed so that structured learning will also take place. Both adults and children enjoy being in control of the language, recognizing how it is built, and how individuals bring meaning to it.

2.1 Word invention poems: beginnings of words: *Subview – the view from the floor*

Level Lower-intermediate to advanced

Time 25 minutes

Aims To explore the meanings and uses of prefixes.

Preparation

1 Choose the prefixes which your students will know from column A and write these on the board or on a classroom poster. Columns B and C are completed for your information, but you will build up these examples during the lesson, with your class, so these columns should be left blank.

A Prefix	B Example	C Meaning
super-	supervisor, superhighway	above, high
super-	supermarket	big
sub-	subway, substandard	under
pre-	preview, premonition	before
co-/con-	co-operate, conversation	with
re-	repeat, reread, redo, revise	again

2   Check **prefix** in the glossary.

Procedure

1   Ask your students to look at the list of prefixes on the board. Invite them to give you examples of words that begin with these prefixes. Write their examples up in column B.

2   Discuss with your students what each set of examples might have in common, and how this knowledge might help you to understand the meaning of the prefix. Write some possible meanings in Column C.

3   Introduce the idea of experimenting with word-building. Tell students to look at the words beginning with the prefix *pre-*. Ask them to substitute the prefix *pre-* with *sub-* to create new words.

Use class ideas to write some examples on the board, along with their definition. Read out with the class the words and their definition, for example:

subview – the view you have when lying on the floor
superoperate – working with someone by acting as their boss

4   Divide your class into groups of two or three. Ask each group to choose one of the prefixes from the blackboard, or another of their choice.

Their task is to create as many 'new' words as possible, using their chosen prefix. Give the class five minutes to write out as many words as they can.

5   Now ask them to write a short definition for each of their invented words. They can prepare poems made up of verses containing three or four invented words and their definitions.

More advanced groups could use the example poems below as a model to write their own 'prefix' poems, experimenting with their words in the way these poets do.

6   When the groups have finished their poems, invite them to read them back to the rest of the class.

Superman

I drive my car to supermarket,
The way I take is superhigh,
A superlot is where I park it,
And Super Suds are what I buy.

Supersalesmen sell me tonic –
Super-Tone-O, for Relief.
The planes I ride are supersonic.
In trains, I like the Super Chief.

Supercilious men and women
Call me superficial – me,
Who so superbly learned to swim in
Supercolossality.

Superphosphate-fed-foods feed me;
Superservice keeps me new.
Who would dare to supersede me,
Super-super-superwho?

John Updike

1984

I'm unapproved, unbeknown,
Uncared for, uncredited,
Undecided, uneducated,
Unequal, unessential,
Unfamed, unfashionable,
Unfortunate, unfunded,
Unhappy, unhoused,
Unimportant, unloved,
Unknowable, unmerited,
Unnoticed, unpractical,
Unrefined, unremembered,
Unsatisfactory, unsheltered,
Unsophisticated, untaught,
Untrained, unversed:
UNEMPLOYED!

Alison Fell (aged 14)

Variations

1 Here is an interesting variation, which has worked well, although it involves more preparation. Prepare a set of cards as follows:

  • ten cards, each with a prefix written on it (*co-, sub-, super-, under-, re-*)
  • 20 cards, each with a word written on it that is able to combine with the prefixes (*way, market, take, operate, worker, pass, write, author*)

Divide the class into two teams, and give each team half the pack of cards: five prefix cards and ten word cards.

Their task is to arrange the cards into as many correct combinations as they can in ten minutes. The winning team is the one with the most correct combinations (*co-operate, co-author, underpass, undertake*).

2 A 'poetic' extension of this, for more advanced classes, would be to invite other fantasy combinations, and ask the team to provide a credible 'meaning' for their invented word. The winning team is the one with the highest number of interesting and credible inventions.

Comments

You may find that some prefix words you find simply don't seem to have a shared meaning. What happens if you can't find the meaning of a prefix?

Check the prefix in a good English–English dictionary. Many dictionaries are very helpful at explaining what prefixes mean, as well as offering examples. If the prefix is not there and there seems to be no connecting meaning in the words you have chosen, it could be the case that the words have very different origins. You could offer this to your students as a possible explanation.

English has so many origins: Anglo-Saxon, French, Greek, and Latin, that sometimes the patterns just don't work!

Sometimes words that appear to have the same prefix, in fact have entirely different meanings:

post – meaning *after*, as in *post-date, postpone*
post – meaning *the mail*, as in *postman, post office*

Allow your discussion to take account of these differences.

2.2 Word invention poems: ends of words
Powerful mice

Level Intermediate to upper-intermediate

Time 25 minutes

Aims To practise using the suffixes -*ful* and -*less*.

Preparation

1 This task is likely to bring out many subtleties in the meanings of words which are grammatical opposites, but not true opposites in meaning.

Before the class, check some of these meanings in the dictionary. Below are a few examples:

careful = giving attention and thought to what you are doing
careless = not giving enough attention or thought to what you are doing

thankful = pleased about something good that has happened, or something bad that has not happened. A person is thankful, a situation cannot be
thankless = unpleasant or difficult to do and unlikely to bring you any rewards or thanks from anyone. A situation is thankless, a person cannot be

thoughtful = showing signs of careful thought; showing that you care for other people
thoughtless = not caring about the possible effects of your words or actions on other people

The following pairs of adjectives are true opposites in meaning:

powerful: powerless
harmful: harmless

You may wish to choose pairs like these with less advanced students.

2 Check **suffix** in the glossary.

Procedure

1 Write the following words on the blackboard.

power	
thought	
thank	
hope	
care	
harm	
-ful	*-less*
thoughtful	thoughtless

2 Ask the students to copy the two suffixes *-ful* and *-less* from the blackboard. Explain that these are headings for two boxes of words.

Ask them to write into the boxes each of the words in the list above, adding the suffix to the end.

Do an example with the students and write it into the boxes.

hopeful   hopeless
thankful   thankless

Discussion questions:

What does each word mean? *Thoughtful* means 'full of thought', so what does *thoughtless* mean?

3 When all the words have been written into the boxes, ask each learner to choose ONE pair of words, for example, *powerful/powerless*.

Ask them to write down three things which the *-ful* word can describe, for example:

An elephant is powerful
A mother is powerful
Study is powerful

Then ask them to write down three things which the *-less* word can describe, for example:

A mouse is powerless
A baby is powerless
Dreaming is powerless

The *-ful* list is verse 1.
The *-less* list is verse 2.

4 Ask the students to read their verses to others in their group. If they like, they can add or change their verses.

5 Now the class is going to experiment with verses 1 and 2.

Experiment A

Choose one line from verse 1, and one line from verse 2. Write them down in pairs.

Do this until all your lines are used up.

An elephant is powerful.
A mouse is powerless.

Experiment B

Choose one line from verse 1. Then repeat the line, but change the *-ful* word to *-less*. Write the two lines in pairs.

Do this until all your lines are used up.

An elephant is powerful.
An elephant is powerless.

More advanced groups could add a line in between each, which begins *because …*

An elephant is powerful
because it is the king of animals.
An elephant is powerless
because it can never hide.

6 Ask each group to choose the poems they like best, and perform them. Half the group could read the *-ful* lines and the other half could read the *-less* lines.

Comments

Check accuracy in the meaning and form of the adjectives. Typical errors are:

- *-ful* spelt with a double *ll*: *thoughtfull*
- adjectives are taken to be exact opposites in meaning.

If students are not sure about meanings, ask them to use a good English dictionary. You could also ask them to work in groups and share their understanding of different words.

2.3 Grammar play poems:
Honeying the girls

Level Lower-intermediate to advanced

Time 25 minutes

Aims To use morphemes to build new words or to change the meaning of existing words.

Preparation

1 Prepare the blackboard plan below by choosing words in Columns A and B which your class will know, and add others of your own to the list.

A Colours	B Food	C	D
red	ice cream	add *-ing*	add *-ly* or *-ily*
pink	cherries		
green	honey		
brown	cheese		
orange	bread		
white	rice	add *-ed*	
grey	egg		
	butter		
	pear		
	marmalade		

2 Check **morpheme** in the glossary.

Procedure

1 Write the blackbord plan on the board. Ask students to look at the words in Columns A and B and suggest more words of their own.

2 Now ask them to look at the endings (or morphemes) in Columns C and D. What happens when these endings are attached to words in Columns A and B? Elicit some ideas from your class, and write these on the board.

The following table offers some examples that may help you. The words in Columns C and D are invented ones, the kind poets create, using morphemes as building blocks.

A Colours	B Food	C *Make a verb*	D *Make an adverb*
red	ice cream	**add -ing**	**add -ly or -ily**
pink	cherries	icecreaming	eggily
green	honey	honeying	cheesily
brown	cheese	cherrying	pinkly
orange	bread	egging	brownly
white	rice	reddening	ice-creamily
grey	egg	browning	
	butter	oranging	
	pear	**add -ed**	
	marmalade	cheesed	
		riced	
		breaded	
		pinked	

3 When you have written a few examples in each of the columns C and D, ask students to find a title for each column. Suggested titles are:

Column C: Make a verb OR Turn words into verbs
Column D: Make an adverb OR Turn words into adverbs

4 Now invite students to make up some words of their own. Write their suggestions on the blackboard. Choose two or three of their examples which are particularly funny or interesting. Ask the class to suggest what these words mean. For example:

honeying: talking nicely to someone to get something you want
cherrying: just going from one happy nice thing to another avoiding everything difficult
pinkly: in a very shy way

5 Ask students to work in groups of two and three. Each group should make up four or five words of their own, then write a short explanation or definition after each word. For example, *marmaladed: spread with jam; or when something delicious happens to you.*

6 After ten minutes, invite each group to read back their list of words and definitions. Ask them to listen to one another:

- to see if others have invented the same words
- to see if others have the same or different definitions
- to create sentences with one another's words.

Below are examples of the invented words used to create group poems.

Summer poem

Summer and time
For honeying the girls

Summer and time
For cherrying

Winter poem

Winter uglies me
In winter I go to work brownly
Like slush

National Poetry Day workshop for teachers: International House

Follow-up

Ask students for homework to find out which of their invented words are really used in English. They can be encouraged

- to use English–English dictionaries
- to ask native speakers
- to find out from one another and/or from more advanced students
- to use dictionaries of idioms.

Comments

The examples in this activity will lead your students to invent words. With less advanced students, you may wish to work only with real words.

The following are examples of real words which can be generated from the suggested list:

to brown (*browned, browning*): used to describe cooking gently, for example, *brown the onions in a pan.*

greyly: in a dull fashion

to butter (*buttered, buttering*): to spread butter on bread

to egg someone on: to encourage someone, to push someone to do something

to be cheesed off: to be bored, unhappy, irritated

Some colours can also become verbs, by adding *-en* to the end:

to whiten
to redden

2.4 Opposites poems: *Idlis and chapattis*

Level   Intermediate to upper-intermediate

Time   25 minutes

Aims   To practise vocabulary of opposites.

Preparation

1   You may want to have the following example on a worksheet or poster to share with students before or after this activity.

> **I and You**
>
> I am the youngest of six
> You are the oldest of five
> I am shy
> You are bossy
> I like bossy people
> You like shy people
> So we are best friends.
>
> I like idli
> You like chapattis
> I like champagne
> You are a teetotaler
> I read Shakespeare
> you love computers
> we are poles apart
>
> but if our worlds come together
> Elysium is born
>
> *Indian students at Chidambaram, India*

2   Prepare the board plan. There will be two columns, A and B. Choose in each column words and phrases which your class will find helpful, as a starting point for the lesson. You will build up more examples during the lesson.

A I	B You
am shy	are friendly
read books	read comics
hate football	love football
live in the West	live in the East
write letters	write emails
remember birthdays	forget birthdays
like ...	like ...

3   Check **antonym** and **paradox** in the glossary.

Procedure

1 Write on the blackboard in two columns:

I   You

Ask the class to look at this, and, if you have prepared this, to read the poem aloud with you.
Tell them the *I* and the *You* are best friends. Ask them:

Are you surprised that they are best friends? If so, why? or why not?

They may say:

because the friends seem to be opposites
they like different things
they are opposite kinds of people
people often like friends who are very different from themselves

2 Ask them to suggest other 'pairs' of opposites, and write these on the board. It may help them to think about real people and friends who are different from them. You may want to suggest that only positive sentiments can be used.

The opposites below have been helpful in classes.

I am	You are
tall	short
quiet	loud
good-tempered	bad-tempered
funny	serious
polite	rude
friendly	shy
youngest	oldest

3 After five minutes, read the sentences on the board with the class. You could read them in one of these patterns: an *I* sentence, then a *You* sentence or all the *I* sentences, then all the *You* sentences. For example:

> I am funny
>   You are serious
>   I am friendly
>   You are shy

OR

I am the youngest
I am short
I am quiet

You are the oldest
You are tall
You are very noisy

4 Now ask the class to work in pairs. Each pair should draw up a list of ways in which they are opposites, using the examples on the board to help them. The list should be a set of sentences: *I/You I/You.*

5 When they have listed five or six differences, ask the partners to write a final sentence which begins:

We both …

6 Invite the partners to share their poems with others in the class.

Variation

A variation of this activity that has worked very well involves:

- *looking at opposites within myself*
- *looking at opposites within my best friend/a loved one*

Ask your class to write pairs of sentences:

I am + adjective
I am + the opposite adjective

The poem below is an example of opposites within an animal.

> My bull is dark like the raincloud in storm
> He is like summer and winter.
> Half of him is dark like the storm cloud
> Half of him is light like the morning star
>
> (*My Magnificent Bull* translated from the Dinka)

Adult learners may enjoy thinking about the idea of **paradox**: that two opposite things can exist side by side in a person, or in a situation.

Comments

Some students may try to create opposites by adding the suffix *-less*, for example, *shy – shyless.*

Explain that many adjectives do take this ending, but many also do not.

Not all adjectives have 'true' opposites. In many cases, your students will need to search in a dictionary for words which are opposite in meaning. In some cases there could be several possible opposites, for example:

> *shy* opposites could be: *outgoing, loud, friendly*
> *serious* opposites could be: *funny, humorous*
> *lively* opposites could be: *slow, quiet*

2.5 Preposition poems: *Water everywhere*

Level Lower-intermediate to advanced

Time 20 minutes

Aims To look at the way a word can combine with different prepositions and to practise prepositional phrases of place.

Materials

- The picture at the beginning of this activity.
- The poem by Valerie Bloom, either prepared to read aloud in the lesson, or copied on a poster or worksheet so your students can read this with you.

Preparation

Copy columns A, B, and C on to the board or on to a classroom poster.

A	B	C
There's	water air noise music sun	in the on the under the over the through the between the

1 Ask your class to look at the picture at the beginning of this activity, and tell you where the water is going, using the phrases on the board.

For example:

There's water down the stairs
There's water under the door
There's water in the street

2 Next read aloud the poem below with your students, and ask them to compare their ideas with these.

> There's water on the ceiling
> And water on the wall,
> There's water in the bedroom,
> And water in the hall,
> There's water on the landing,
> And water on the stair,
> Whenever daddy takes a bath,
> There's water everywhere.
>
> *Valerie Bloom*

3 Divide the class into groups of three and four, and ask each group to choose a word from the list in Column B, or find one of their own.

4 Ask the groups to write at least six lines, with the key word in each line. The prepositions on the blackboard can be used as many times as necessary. Below is an example:

> There's noise on the street
> there's noise inside my head
> there's noise in the houses
> there's noise in the shops
> there's noise between people
> there's noise on the radio
> there's noise instead of silence
> there's noise instead of peace
>
> *Classroom poem: Plymouth Creative English class*

5 After ten minutes, ask the groups to plan a performance of their lines. The 'cascade' method would be an exciting way of reading these lines:

One student, or group of students, reads line 1.
Before line 1 is finished, a second group of students reads line 2.
Before line 2 is finished, a third group of students reads line 3.

Thus, the lines read as a kind of cacophony of noise – just what they are describing.

> Noise: it's in the streets
> Noise: it's in the corridors
> Noise: it's in my head

2.6 Word association poems: *Red, the money goddess*

Level Intermediate to advanced

Time 25 minutes

Aims To look at the positive or negative connotations of words and sounds and to explore the cultural information contained in words.

Materials

A list of the words in stage 1 of the Preparation below, either on a blackboard, on a poster, or on a worksheet copied for your class.

Preparation

1 In the box below are some words which often appear in myths, nursery tales, and stories worldwide. Add to these, change them, make your own list, so the words are ones which your students will know, and which will match the stories they may remember from childhood.

Your students will need to see a copy of your chosen list of words.

fountain	rose	crow	dog	dove
apple	island	thorn	wolf	fox
tree	snake	dragon	wizard	witch
bird	spring	seven	three	red
white	sun	moon	night	star

2 Check **connotation** in the glossary.

Procedure

1 Ask your students to look at the words. Make sure they understand what all the words mean. Then invite them to choose which words they 'like', or which are GOOD, POSITIVE, PLEASANT, and which they don't 'like' or which are BAD, NEGATIVE, UNPLEASANT. Encourage them to use their gut feelings to respond to the words, and not to think too hard.

2 After two minutes, elicit some answers from the class: *Which words did you like? / not like? Were there any different opinions? Can you explain why?*

like	**not like**
fountain	*crow*
rose	*dog*
dove	

Here are some reasons why your students might feel positive or negative about the words. Encourage them to discuss all these possibilities:

- because of the sound of the word
- because the word reminds them of another which has a positive/negative meaning
- because of a personal experience connected with this object
- because of a story, myth, nursery tale connected with this object

3   Ask students to work on their own for five minutes. They should divide a blank sheet of paper into two columns: POSITIVE/NEGATIVE.

Under each column, they should choose words from the list which match.

Positive	Negative
rose	*thorn*
crow	*dove*

4   When they have finished, ask students to work in groups of three or four to compare their lists.

What differences were there? What similarities? Can you explain why?

5   Ask them to record their feelings about the words in groups. From the list, they should choose five words which were particularly interesting. Maybe everyone felt the same about this word but for different reasons, or everyone felt differently about the word. Their task is to write the word and beside it to write a short definition, or description, of each person's feeling about the word. For example:

red:
dangerous, like blood,
brave, like courage

6   When each group has written at least three words with their descriptions, invite them to read their lines aloud in class.

You may wish to add the following examples to your classroom reading:

Red
dangerous, like blood
beautiful like a wedding sari
wealth, it's the face of the money goddess

White
it is pure, a burial gown
the colour of ashes
the colour of the water lily
big on water

Group poems by Indian students in Chidambaram

3

Wordmixing poems

It has often been said that the heart of poetic language is the way it makes comparisons which are strange and unlikely, comparisons which throw a completely new and surprising light on everyday things. Poetry can bring to life inanimate things, like a city, a storm, or a sea shell. It can make them appear to have human qualities, as in *the snorting storm*, or it can take something intangible like a feeling or an idea, and turn it into something we can almost see, such as, *hope like a spoon*.

This chapter reminds us that words are not isolated but more like colours that change according to their neighbours. Red next to yellow leaps out; red next to brown disappears. It is the same with words. Compare, for example, how the words below change according to the company they keep:

cherry tree family tree shoe tree

the blue sea feeling blue singing the blues

Other words seem to come in pairs. When we break them up, one of the halves seems to make no sense at all. For example:

spick and span means clean and bright, but what does *spick* mean?
to and fro means back and forwards, but what does *fro* mean?

A comparison with colours may also be drawn in this case. Yellow and red need to be mixed to make orange. The two colours combine to make something new.

This chapter shows students how they can use words, like colours, to paint pictures of their own. The activities invite the students to describe their feelings about favourite objects, friends and family, places, and pictures. They do this by mixing and combining words in unusual ways, by making ideas so visible we can see them, by making inanimate things seem to breathe, and by making descriptions leap out like the colour red.

3.1 Similes about language learning: *Words like sea shells*

Level   Lower-intermediate to advanced

Time   25 minutes

Aims   To give students an opportunity to describe language learning. To use the phrases *like* and *as ... as* – to make comparisons.

Preparation

Check **simile** in the glossary.

Procedure

1   Ask your class to tell you what they would like to do now instead of being in class. List their ideas on the blackboard as *-ing* structures:

dancing
playing the guitar
sleeping
lying on the beach

2   Now write the following phrase at the top of the blackboard:

Learning a language is like ...

Below is an example of what the blackboard might look like at this stage of the lesson:

Learning a language is like . . .

climbing a mountain
swimming an ocean
collecting sea shells
polishing stones
wind-surfing
climbing a mountain
playing the guitar
listening to music
sleeping
surfing the internet

---

3   Invite the students to try out the different *-ing* phrases to finish the sentence and suggest to you the combinations they like best.

4   Now invite students to work in groups of two and three and finish the phrase in four different ways. Each sentence is a line of their poem.

With more advanced students you could also add other phrases, such as those suggested below.

Learning new words is like ...
Learning grammar is like ...

5 After ten minutes invite the students to share their completed sentences with a neighbour. You may also like to share with them the example below.

> Learning new words
> is like climbing a mountain
> collecting stones on the way
> polishing them
> putting them in your pocket
> so your journey is slow
>
> the stones are heavy
> but when you reach home
> some of the mountain is still with you
>
> I collect words like sea shells.
> Each one is different.
> They are
> white, pink, grey,
> many colours.
> I remember places I have visited.
>
> *Class poem: Chinese students in Oxford*

3.2 Similes about people: *Sister like a flower*

Level Intermediate to advanced

Time 25 minutes

Aims To practise ways of describing people in unusual and memorable ways. To practise the use of *like* and *as* to make comparisons and to revise the use of countable and uncountable nouns.

Preparation

1 Choose the words in the lists below which your students will
understand and write them on the board.

A Title_____	B Title_____
mother	tree
father	flower
uncle	lake
aunt	river
	stone
	shell
	mountain
	hill

2 Check **countable nouns** and **uncountable nouns** in the glossary.

Procedure

1 Ask your class to look at the two lists on the blackboard. Invite them
to suggest what the words in each column have in common, and to
suggest a title or label for each column. Possible titles might be:

Column A: *people in the family, members of the family, my family*
Column B: *outside the city, nature, in the countryside*

Accept any title you think is helpful and write this at the top of the
list.

2 Divide the class into pairs. Ask Partner A to write down as many
words as he/she can for Column A. Ask Partner B to write down as
many words as he/she can for Column B. After five minutes stop the
class and ask the partners to compare their two lists of words.

Below are some ideas which have been helpful in this activity. The
list of people can also grow to include friends, neighbours, and other
people in your students' lives.

father	sand
mother	rock
grandmother	stone
grandfather	ice
cousin	a river
aunt	the sea
uncle	a leaf
neighbour	fruit: a pear, an orange,
best friend	a kiwi fruit, a mango
teacher	
school friends	
husband	
wife	
girlfriend	
boyfriend	

3 From the list ask the partners to match words from the two lists which are like each other. Ask them to make at least four matches.

my father is like a rock
my mother is like a lake
my sister is like a flower

4 Beside each pair of words ask them to write a short explanation. For example:

My father is like a rock. He never moves.
My mother is like a lake. She changes when the weather changes.

Below are examples you might want to share with your class.

> My little brother is like the pepper flower.
> He makes me laugh.
> He jumps out at me, in the field,
> with a red hat.
>
> My father is like a rock.
> His chin is sharp.
> He looks at me from the top of a mountain.
> He is very old.
>
> My mother is like a lake.
> I see my face in her.
> She changes when the weather changes.
> I change when the weather changes.
>
> *Malaysian students in Plymouth*

Comments

Less advanced students may find the explanations difficult. For these groups encourage the similes only. Here is a list without explanations generated by one class:

my brother is like jumping rain
my sister is like a flower behind a tree

The main language point in this activity is whether to use an article and if so which one. Some of the nouns in the list take a DEFINITE article or none at all because they are uncountable. For example:

my sister is like the sky
my friend is like water

Others can be counted and so take an INDEFINITE article in the singular. For example:

my mother is like a river
my teacher is like a tree

Take note of whether your students use articles correctly and can see a difference between the countable nouns and the uncountable ones. Invite them to experiment with turning words into the plural and adding numbers:

Ten skies? NO! Uncountable
Ten rivers? YES! Countable

3.3 Idiom poems: *As dear as a donkey*

Level   Intermediate to advanced

Time   25 minutes

Aims   To practise the typical idiom structure: *as ... as* and to compare different cultures' expressions and idioms.

Preparation

1   Prepare the plan below to share with your class.

Column A	Column B
as mad as	a cucumber
as sweet as	sugar
as cool as	a button
as good as	gold
as bright as	a March hare

2   Check **idioms** and **alliteration** in the glossary.

Procedure

1   Write the plan on the board and ask your students to look at the list of phrases. Explain that these are idioms but the second halves are all jumbled up. Can they guess what the second halves should be?

2   Invite your students to join the correct halves together with lines on the blackboard. The correct answers are below along with several other idioms your class may enjoy.

as mad as	a March hare
as sweet as	sugar
as cool as	a cucumber
as good as	gold
as pleased as	punch
as happy as	a sandboy
as bright as	a button
as deaf as	a post
as blind as	a bat
as dull as	ditchwater
as stubborn as	a mule

3   Ask the class to explain why they think the combinations are appropriate. They may say that some of them have the same sounds in both halves, for example, *cool – cucumber, bright – button.*

4   Ask if there are any similar idioms or expressions in their mother tongue. Invite them to translate directly from their language and write the new idioms on the blackboard. When you have a list of idioms read these out with the class.

5 Now write the following on the board: *as … as … .*

Explain the students' task now is to write their own idioms. Ask your class to work in groups of two and three and write as many 'idioms' as they can in ten minutes.

6 After ten minutes invite the groups to read their lists to one another. You may also wish to share with them this example:

> as pleased as a pony
> as dear as a donkey
> as happy as a sunflower
> as bright as a mirror
> as fresh as a fountain
> as strong as a stone

Classroom poem, St. Gallen, Switzerland

Follow-up

For homework the class could find out as many new idioms as they can in English which begin *as … as …*

Variations

A variation of this activity is to prepare a pack of about 24 cards. Write on each card one half of an idiom:

As happy as   a sandboy

Divide the class into two teams, shuffle the cards, and hand out half the pack to each team. Their task could be one of the following:

- put the cards together into as many correct combinations as you can in ten minutes
- make as many new and exciting combinations as you can in ten minutes with a brief explanation of what your new idiom means
- write your own other halves to the labels you have. A set of blank labels could be used for the team to write their 'other halves'.

Comments

Some of the idioms cannot be explained by looking at their two halves. For example: who can explain what *Punch* means in *as pleased as Punch*? or what a *sandboy* is in *happy as a sandboy*? Most native speakers will not be able to tell you the answers to these questions.

The interesting thing about an idiom is that it changes and evolves over such a long period of time that often we forget how the idiom started. There are several things you as a teacher can do about this:

- explain to your students that idioms have a very long history and are thus difficult to explain
- ask them to collect the difficult ones and check the meaning in a dictionary
- find out the 'story' of the idiom from one of the suggested books in the bibliography and explain it to your students
- explain that idioms have to be learnt as a whole chunk and cannot be changed, divided up, or analysed part by part.

3.4 Adjective/noun poems: *The kind snow*

Level Lower-intermediate to advanced

Time 25 minutes

Aims To experiment with different combinations of adjectives and nouns and to look at how meaning is changed when words are connected in different ways.

Preparation

1 To develop the activity into individual and group student writing you will need to:
   - plan the best way to divide your class into four to six groups, depending on the size of your class
   - write one label for each group for the group leader to read aloud.

   Here are examples of the labels.

GROUP 1 Write as many ADJECTIVES as you can which describe PEOPLE (*kind, funny, clever*)	GROUP 4 Write as many NOUNS as you can which describe MEMBERS OF A FAMILY (*mother, father*)
GROUP 2 Write as many COLOURS as you can (*red, green, brown, purple*)	GROUP 5 Write as many NOUNS as you can which describe WEATHER (*sun, rain, storm*)
GROUP 3 Write as many ADJECTIVES as you can which describe SHAPE AND SIZE (*big, small, round, curvy*)	GROUP 6 Write as many NOUNS as you can which describe PLACES (*city, mountain, desert, village*)

Each member of the group will need to make a record of their work, so make sure they all have paper and pens.

Dictionaries may also be helpful if your class are familiar with using them.

2 Check **adjectives, nouns** and **lexical sets** in the glossary.

Procedure

1   Write the following phrases on the board: *the happy uncle, the black storm, the lonely village, the rude desert, the kind snow*. Ask your class to look at the phrases and try to spot a pattern. Try to elicit:

adjective noun

Don't worry however if this is not elicited. The next stage will help you to elicit the explanation.

2   Rub out the adjectives in one or two of your phrases.

the _____ uncle
the _____ storm

Ask your students to suggest other words you could put in the gap, and write these on the blackboard in a column headed ADJECTIVES (Column A).

3   Now rub out the nouns in one or two phrases.

the lonely _____
the rude _____

Ask your students to suggest words to fill this gap too and write these on the blackboard in a list headed NOUNS (Column B).

Try and elicit five or six examples in each category.

4   Now invite the class to join up the words in Columns A and B in as many different ways as they can. Ask them these questions:

Are there any combinations which sound strange? or interesting?
Are there any words which seem to combine in many ways?
Are there any words which change their meaning when combined with others?

You could share with them the classroom poem below, as an example of strange and interesting combinations.

> the red storm
> the cruel ice
> the lonely village
> the lonely birthday
> the kind snow
> the proud valley
> the friendly sun
> the sweet rain
> the sweet anniversary
>
> *Classroom poem: Totnes School of English*

5   Now divide your class into four or six groups depending on the size of your class. Give each group one of the labels you have prepared. Explain that each member of the group will need to write down as many words as they can in five minutes according to the instructions on the group label. They should write them clearly on small pieces of paper because other groups are going to read their words.

Here is an example of nouns and adjectives which students have suggested.

ADJECTIVES Column A	NOUNS Column B
1 describing a person *happy, sad, lonely, kind, polite, rude, friendly, clever, sweet, cruel, nasty, beautiful*	4 members of the family *father, daughter, cousin, nephew mother-in-law*
2 colours *red, green, brown, orange, pink*	5 weather *storm, snow, ice, frost, rain, sun, showers, monsoon*
3 shape and size *round, square, huge, tiny, triangular, little, fat, thin, slim, stocky, chunky*	6 places *city, village, town, lake, mountain, hill, valley, river, desert*

6   After ten minutes ask the groups to stop work. Take all the pieces of paper in from each group. Keep them carefully in two sets:

Pack 1: all the adjectives
Pack 2: all the nouns

7   Shuffle each pack and give each group:

a handful of adjectives
a handful of nouns

8   Now invite each group to spread all the words out between them in two columns:

ADJECTIVES   NOUNS

Their task is to make interesting combinations from the words that they have. The combinations should make sense in some interesting way and should be grammatical in that only adjectives and nouns can be combined (not noun + noun).

Give the groups ten minutes to find as many interesting combinations as they can and write these down as a 'group poem'.

9   After ten minutes ask the groups to read aloud their poems or to write them out and display them on the walls.

Variations

This activity can be used to practise any adjective or noun topics you have studied in class. As long as each category 1–6 is different and there are equal numbers of noun and adjective groups, the activity will work well. Below are some topics which have been effective:

adjectives of taste: *sweet, sour, spicy, hot, dry*

adjectives of texture/feel: *hard, spiky, furry, soft, smooth*

adjectives of temperature: *hot, lukewarm, tepid, cool, warm*

transport: *bus, car, taxi, train, plane, bicycle, air balloon*

animals (including fish and insects): *tiger, cat, mouse, lion, salmon, spider*

rites of passage: *birthday, anniversary, graduation, marriage, confirmation, school-days, youth, adulthood, old age*

family members: *mother, father, sister, uncle, cousin*

Comments

Sometimes your students may put together noun + noun instead of adjective + noun.

You could explain that many adjectives can be changed from a noun to an adjective by adding *-y*

storm stormy
rain rainy
cloud cloudy

However you may be surprised how many noun + noun combinations work very well indeed, for example: *city father, snow queen, river valley, ice storm.*

Upper-intermediate students engaged in this task have pointed out this extra dimension to the task. This 'noun + noun' poem was produced by one of these classes:

> the village mother
> the city father
> the city storm
> the village storm
> the snow mother
> the ice father
>
> *Hungarian students, Pecs*

Allow any combinations which make sense, are interesting, and are grammatically possible.

3.5 Metaphor poems: *Hope is a spoon*

Level Intermediate to advanced

Time 25 minutes

Aims To develop vocabulary and to experiment with making unusual comparisons.

Preparation

Check **metaphor, abstract noun,** and **concrete noun** in the glossary.

Procedure

1 Write on the blackboard two or three words from the list below which your students understand.

> knife, eggs, spoon, cheese, plate, bed, wood

2 Ask your students to look at these words. Where would you find all these objects? Ask the students to write five more words of their own for things/objects which are in their homes.

3 While the students are writing, draw this chart on the blackboard. Add words of your own to Column A which your students might understand and enjoy.

A	B	C
Love		a/an ...
Hope		
Kindness		
Unkindness		
Time	is	
Age		
Fire		
Anger		

4 Now ask the students to finish the sentences by filling in household words in Column C. Do some examples with the students.

For example:

Time is an egg.
Fire is a knife.
Hope is a spoon.

5 Ask the students to ask the question *Why?*

- Why is time like an egg?
- Why is fire like a knife?
- Why is hope like a spoon?

Write down some of their answers on the blackboard. For example:

Fire is a knife.	*Hope is a spoon.*	*Time is an egg.*
It cuts down.	*It holds.*	*It breaks.*
	It feeds.	*It gives birth.*

Here are some words which may be useful. They can be used to describe both the domestic objects and the concepts listed on the board.

Verbs	Adjectives
cuts	sharp
breaks	firm
holds	strong
serves	kind
slices	comfortable
feeds	delicious
comforts	useful
	dangerous

6 Now ask your students to work in groups of two or three and to write verses with three lines each:

Their comparison: *Anger is a knife.*
Two reasons: *It cuts. It is sharp.*

7 Ask students to share their ideas in pairs and groups.
They can help each other to finish, change, or add to their verses.
When they are ready invite them to:

- read their poem aloud to the class
- write it on a poster and put it on the wall
- include it in a class anthology.

Comments

This task is about comparisons and the meaning of words. The main questions to ask when checking written work are:

Do the comparisons work? Are the verbs and adjectives used equally true of the domestic object and of the human experience? If they are not, you could suggest others which are, or ask students to work with one another to make suggestions.

3.6 Weather poems: *The snorting storm*

Level Intermediate to advanced

Time 25 minutes

Aims To look at words which apply to living things and words which do not apply to living things and to explore the effect of mixing up these words.

Materials
- The picture on the next page.
- The poems in this activity, prepared to share with your students.

Preparation

1 Prepare the board with the chart below, writing just the headings and two or three examples from each box. Choose words the students will be familiar with. You will be eliciting from the students other words for each box. However these might help you if they run out of ideas.

A Weather	B Animals
rain monsoon storm thunder fog mist drizzle snow blizzard hail winds sunshine drought	cat pig snake horse bull lion butterfly rabbit

C What does the animal DO?

flies flutters snores snorts purrs slithers slides grunts butts chases gallops roars runs leaps bounces sits

2 Check **personification** in the glossary.

Procedure

1 Ask students to look at the picture and tell you:

What does the horse sound like?
What does the rain sound like?
Can you suggest a phrase or a sentence to explain what the people can hear?

Example answers are:

The rain, like a horse on a tin roof
The hooves of the rain
The rain galloped across the roof …

2 Ask students to suggest to you other ANIMAL and WEATHER words and write these on the board in Columns A and B.
Then ask them to suggest words for what each animal does – how they move, eat, make noises. Write their suggestions in Box C on the blackboard.

3 *If each kind of* WEATHER *was an* ANIMAL, *what would it be?*

What would it do?

Elicit students' ideas and write sentences on the board to record their suggestions.

The storm is like a horse. It snorts.
The fog is like a snake. It slithers.

4 Now students can form groups of two or three. Each group should choose one type of weather and one type of animal. Ask them to list as many ways as possible in which the weather behaves like the animal.

Below are two examples from student workshops.

> Rain
> bounces on the street
> chases children
> leaps off the umbrella
> sits in black puddles
> runs into gutters
> like a hare.
>
> The storm,
> It snorts.
> It grunts.
> It gallops,
> It roars
> like a horse.

Classroom poems: language students in Totnes and Switzerland

Follow-up

More advanced students may be interested to discuss the use of language here in more detail.

All the verbs are usually used to describe something living – a person or an animal. What happens when you use these words to describe the weather instead? What happens to our idea of the weather?

Prepare the poem below for your students and ask them to notice how the fog has turned into a cat, or has the cat turned into the fog?! *Which verbs describe the cat? Which verbs describe the fog?*

> The yellow fog that rubs its back upon the window-panes
> The yellow smoke that rubs its muzzle on the window-
>   panes,
> Licked its tongue into the corner of the evening,
> Lingered upon the pools that stand in drains,
> Let fall upon its back the soot that falls from chimneys,
> Slipped by the terrace, made a sudden leap,
> And, seeing that it was a soft October night,
> Curled once about the house and fell asleep.

T.S. Eliot from The Love Song of Alfred J. Prufrock

4

Sentence pattern poems

This chapter looks at different sentence types:
- short or simple sentences with one clause or main verb only
- complex sentences with more than one main verb
- questions
- exclamations
- commands or orders

It is a pleasant discovery for students to realize that some sentence types are complete with just one word only.

Stop! (Imperative)
Aha! (Exclamation)

A great deal can be said with one-word utterances like these and even whole conversations can be conducted this way. Activities 4.3 and 4.4 are both examples of how students can do this.

Even the longer and more difficult sentence types can be made simpler by using frames on which to hang meanings. With these frames, even language learners at the early stages will have ways of expressing interesting ideas.

This chapter also looks at how sentences can be broken up into chunks and what happens when these chunks are moved around. Activity 4.7 shows what students can do simply with short phrases: *surprised by, pleased by, confused by*. It is possible to use these phrases as building blocks, moving them around, or lifting them out of sentences altogether. How many changes can we make to a sentence and still ensure it makes sense? How much can we 'play' with word order and still keep a sentence grammatical? Activity 4.8 gives students the opportunity to ask and answer this question and at the same time to generate surprising new sentences of their own.

4.1 *I can, I can't: I can hear the rain*

Level Lower-intermediate to intermediate

Time 25 minutes

Aims To practise the negative form and to contrast statements and negative sentences (*I can, I can't*).

Preparation

1 Copy the blackboard plan. Choose the phrases which your students will understand from columns A and B.

A	B
I can taste	I can't taste
I can see	I can't see
I can hear	I can't hear

2 Check **modals** in the glossary.

Procedure

1 Ask your class to look at the phrases in Column A and suggest words to end each sentence. *What can they hear/see/feel?* Write their examples on the board.

2 Now ask your students to think about things they cannot do because they are far away, or because they are unable or forbidden to. Ask them to suggest words to end each sentence in Column B, and write these on the board in Column C.

Here are some answers suggested by students.

A	B	C
I can see I can hear	I can't see I can't hear	friends, parents, classmates (people) houses, streets, cities, towns, cars, shops, countryside, villages, the sea (places) books, blackboard, pictures, windows, paper, paints, dictionaries (classroom objects)
I can taste I can smell	I can't taste I can't smell	goat's cheese, mangoes, olives (food)

3 Invite the class to read out the sentences they have suggested. These could be 'performed' in several ways:

half the class reads all the *can* sentences, then
half the class reads all the *can't* sentences

Or alternate: one *can* sentence, one *can't* sentence

4 Now ask students to write verses of their own.

Each verse should have four lines. Each line should be a *can* or a *can't* sentence, but the students can make up their own patterns (or you could suggest a pattern). For example:

Pattern 1   **Pattern 2**
1 *can* line   1 *can* line
1 *can't* line   1 *can't* line
1 *can* line   1 *can't* line
1 *can't* line   1 *can't* line

5 When the students have finished their verse, ask them to share their poems with others in the group. If they wish they can make a group poem using all their verses. Ask them to read these back to the class or make a class anthology.

6 You could also share the classroom poem below with your students. The poem has some errors in it but do you think these are important? If they corrected these errors, would the poem be better?

> I can hear the rain water
> I can't hear the sea water
> I can hear my teacher talking
> I can't hear my parents talking
> I can see my class friends laughing
> I can't see my brother playing
> I can see the no colour sky
> I can't feel the sun weather of my country
>
> *Lines from Malaysian and Turkish students*

Variations

Other negative/positive patterns work well with this activity:

I know … I don't know …
I want … I don't want …

You could also practise the form below, which avoids repeating the verb twice:

I know … but not …
I want … but not …

This is an example by a Japanese student who has used this pattern:

> I want to look at everything
> but not to look at lonely people
> I want to hear about everything
> but not to hear about lonely people
> I want to talk with everyone
> but not to talk with lonely people
> I want to know about everything
> but not to know about lonely people
>
> *Junko Huzo*

Comments

Typical errors are:

- a double negative (*I can't not*)
- the infinitive of the verb after *can't* (*I can't to do something*)

Allow other kinds of errors, but check that your students have formed the negative correctly.

4.2 Inner questions: *Where are you?*

Level **Lower-intermediate to intermediate**

If you have a mixed ability class, the higher-level students should be Partner A, forming questions.

The lower-level students should be Partner B, forming short sentences using the present continuous.

Time **20 minutes**

Aims **To revise question forms and the present continuous.**

Procedure

1 Ask your class to think about this situation:

You are expecting a friend to arrive who is very important to you. But it is now two hours past the meeting time and your friend has not arrived. What questions would you ask in your mind?

> *Did you miss your bus?*
> *Are you in a traffic jam?*
> *Are you still at work?*
> *Was it difficult to leave your family?*
> *Is one of your children sick?*
> *Has your mobile phone broken?*
> *Have you been stopped by the police?*

2 Write up their questions in one part of the blackboard. When there are five or six questions, read them aloud with the class.

3 Divide the class into pairs and ask the pairs to sit back to back. They are not going to speak to one another until the next stage in the activity.

Explain that each partner is going to write their own 'inner' voice.

Partner A is going to write three or four more questions, wondering where the friend has gone.

Partner B is the friend. Write three or four sentences describing where you could be. Perhaps you are on a dream journey, doing what you would most like to be doing. Use the present continuous structure:

I'm … -ing

4 After five minutes, ask the partners to share their sentences.

Verse 1 includes all the questions
Verse 2 includes all the answers

Below is an example.

> **Verse 1**
> Where are you?
> Who are you with?
> Did you forget our meeting?
>
> **Verse 2**
> I'm swimming in a blue sea.
> I'm playing the guitar under a tree.
> I'm writing a poem in the sunshine with the sea nearby.

5 When they have finished, ask the pairs to read out their lines, each partner reading the voice he/she has written. One interesting technique that has worked to make 'theatre' out of this poem is for the partners to stand at opposite ends of the classroom, so their voices sound far apart.

Variations

Ask partners to make sure the questions are written on one sheet, the answers on another.

Then collect in all the pages, shuffle them, and hand out one question and one answer sheet to each pair randomly.

In this way, a new poem is created. Ask each pair to read aloud their poem.

Comments

A more advanced class might use a range of question forms for this activity:

- Simple present: *Are you OK? Where are you?*
- Present continuous: *Are you playing your guitar under a tree?*
- Simple past: *Did you get lost? Did you forget the bus fare?*

Make sure they don't confuse these three different structures. Typical errors are:

Did you playing your guitar?
Are you forget the bus fare?

4.3 Conversation poems: *OK, bye-bye*

Level Elementary to advanced

Time 20 minutes

Aims To practise exclamations and to notice how much information can be communicated with one-word or two-word exchanges.

Preparation

1 Below is a short 'conversation' using only exclamations. You could copy this on the board or write your own conversation which your class will enjoy.

> A OK?
> B *No.*
> A No?
> B *No!*
> A Why?
> B *Look.*
> A Oh dear.
> B *Yes.*
> A Sorry.

2 Check **exclamation** in the glossary.

Procedure

1 Ask your students to look at the picture at the beginning of this activity.

What information does the speaker give us about his mood?
What information do we get from the punctuation?

More advanced students might like to guess the other half of the conversation and compare their answers in pairs.

2 Write the conversation on the board and ask your students to read it aloud with you.
Invite them to notice the importance of intonation and how this is suggested by the punctuation.

Half the class could read A.
Half the class could read B.

Can they guess what is happening between A and B? What is the 'story'? If your students are beginners, allow them to use the mother tongue to tell you this. If you wish, invite them to give A and B names.

3 Now invite your group to suggest other words and phrases like these and write them on the board. Even beginners might be able to suggest: *yes, no, OK, hi, hello, bye.*

Use the examples below to help.

Praise and agreement	Directions	Greeting, apology, disagreement
Well done!	Over there!	Hi! Hallo!
Great!	Over here!	Cheers!
Terrific!	Here!	No! No?
Lovely!	This way!	Oh!
Yes!	That way!	Oh dear.
Sure!	Look!	Never mind.
OK!		Bye!
		Sorry
		Please!
		Thank you!

4 Ask students to work in groups of two and three. Explain that each group is going to invent a conversation using only the words or phrases on the board. Give them five minutes to write their conversation and to plan the story behind it.

5 After five minutes invite the groups to share their conversations. While the groups listen to one another, invite them to guess each other's stories.

Encourage your students to exaggerate intonation to show the difference between questions, greetings, and exclamations.

For example: *No? No!*
OK? OK!

This difference is very important if the conversations are to make sense.

4.4 Orders and commands: *Stones as souvenirs*

Level   Lower-intermediate to advanced

Time   20 minutes

Aims   To practise the language of rules and regulations. To practise commands with a negative structure: *Do not ...*

Preparation

1   Ask students, for homework before the lesson, to walk round the school/college and copy down three or four official signs that they find. If these are not in English, you could ask them to translate them or translate the signs for them depending on your students' level.

For example:

Push
Pull
No running in the corridor.
Girls only. Boys only.

2   Copy on to the blackboard three or four phrases from the box below, which your students will understand.

Follow the footpath.
Look after your dog.
Do not leave litter.
Close the door after you.
Please turn off the light.

---

3   Check **imperatives** in the glossary.

Procedure

1   Invite your class to look at the rules and regulations you have written on the board. Ask them to suggest where they might see these rules. They might suggest:

in the countryside, in a garden, in a park, on the beach, by the seaside

2   Ask them to suggest other 'rules' which they might find in these places. If they have done the homework task, of collecting signs around the school or college, elicit these and write them on the board.

Below is a list of suggested 'rules'.

Keep your dog on a lead Follow the footpath Close the gate after you Remove shoes before entering	
No smoking No stopping No parking Do not walk on the grass Do not take photographs Do not leave rubbish/litter Do not write on the walls Do not pick the flowers Do not remove the stones Do not run on the beach Do not swim here	

3 Now explain they are going to write new rules for a different situation. Choose a suitable situation for your class. Here are some suggestions.

Rules for growing up
Rules for making and keeping friends
Rules for a marriage
Rules for getting on with your flatmate.

Ask the class to suggest different rules for this new situation. They can use the ideas on the blackboard and just change key words. You could use the poem below as an example, either on the blackboard or on a poster in the classroom.

Keeping friends

Do not take secrets from your friend
Do not run away from your friend
Do not pick her flowers
But if you do, return them carefully.
Do not throw lies at your friend.
Follow her footpath carefully,
And sometimes let her follow yours.
Stay silent, so you can hear the birds' song.
Do not stop. Do not turn back.
Pick stones as souvenirs.

Classroom poems: Hungary and Switzerland

4 Ask your students to work in groups of two and three and write their own 'rules' poem. They can use the situation you have suggested or make up one of their own. After ten minutes invite groups to share their poems with one another. If they have made up new situations, ask them to guess titles for each other's poems.

Variations

An interesting variation, which has worked well, is to reverse all the rules you have on the blackboard. For example:

Smoking!
Leave litter!
Do not push.
Do not pull.

Ask your students to reverse five or six of these rules and then give their list a title. Tell them to imagine what kind of place would have such anti-rules.
Here is an example.

Peace Protest

Do spit.
Do shout.
Do run.
Do talk.
Normal service will not be resumed.
Please do not wait for instructions.
Please do not keep calm.
Please do disturb the bus driver.
Please do stand up.
Please do stand up and be counted.

Teachers' workshop, London

Comments

A rule NOT to do something begins:

Do not + root of the verb (*Do not spit!*)
or
No + *ing* (*No smoking* !)

Take care your students do not confuse these two structures.
Typical errors are:

Do not spitting!
No smoke!

4.5 Relative clauses: *I wonder who paints butterflies*

Level Lower-intermediate to intermediate

Time 20 minutes

Aims To practise the structure *I wonder who/what/why/whether.*

Preparation

1 Choose some of the questions and patterns below and write these on the blackboard as a starting point.

Asking questions about the world

I wonder who chose the colour of butterflies.
I wonder who made all the petals of flowers.
I wonder why sheep have wool.
I wonder why trees live so long.

I wonder	who
	why
	what
	whether
	where

---

2 Check **relative clauses** in the glossary.

Procedure

1 Ask your students to look at your questions on the blackboard. Read them aloud with the students and discuss with them:

What are these questions about?
Does anyone have the answers?
Are there any more questions about the world you would like to ask which have no answers?

2 Ask your students to suggest new questions to add to the list. The questions may fall into one of the two patterns suggested in the table below. Depending on the level of your class, you may want to choose just one of the patterns to practise or both.

I wonder who OR *I wonder why/what/where*

Write their suggestions on the blackboard.

	Pattern	Examples
I wonder who	1 verb + noun	painted spots on ladybirds chose the colour of butterflies made the elephant's long nose
I wonder why	2 noun + verb	tigers have stripes sheep have wool trees live so long
I wonder where		the sun goes at night
I wonder whether		the sea gets tired flowers sleep
I wonder what	Pattern 1 AND Pattern 2	happens to the moon during the day lions do in winter polar bears do in summer

3 Now divide the class into groups of two and three. Ask each group to continue writing four or five new questions, using the patterns you have suggested on the board.

Below is a list of words that may help them to start the second part of the sentence.

names of animals – *tiger, pig, sheep, elephant, cicada*
names of flowers and plants – *rose, cactus*
names of fruit – *cherry, mango, papaya*
names of the seasons – *spring, summer, autumn, winter*

For example:

I wonder why the tiger …
I wonder whether the papaya …
I wonder where the cherry …

4 After 15 minutes ask the partners to share their lines with another group.

You could draw up a class poem, listing all their questions, and display these on the wall.

On the following page there are two more examples you could share with your class.

I wonder why clouds float?
I wonder why water moves?
I wonder why trees live so long?
I wonder why people need sleep?

Creative English class questions, Plymouth

I wonder
who lives
in the sky
way up high
above the clouds

I wonder
what they have
for lunch
and what their
house looks like

I truly wonder
who lives in the sky
way above the clouds
into endless blue space beyond which I cannot see

I wonder
what makes her sad
and why she cries
this rain that
comes from the sky

Opal Palmer Adisa, Jamaica

Comments

Students may confuse the two types of sentence mentioned above:

I wonder why do trees live so long.

If they make sentences of this kind, return to the patterns on the blackboard. In another lesson you may want to return to the direct question form.

4.6 I know poem: *My mother knows my shoe size*

Level Elementary to upper-intermediate

Time 20 minutes

Aims To practise simple sentences using the verb *know + a noun*. To practise complex sentences using *know + a subordinate clause*.

Preparation

1 Copy the following chart on to the board.

```
My sister                    knows
My brother
My father
My mother
My friend
My ...
```

2 Prepare the following poems so that you can display them in the classroom on posters and share them with your students.

> My sister knows I like boys.
> My mother knows I like chocolate.
> My father knows I don't like homework.
>
> My friends know I am funny.
> My mother knows I am lazy.
> My sister knows I am crazy!
>
> *Class poem: Bedford Language Centre children*

> **Another filling**
> My sister knows my name and nothing else.
> My mother knows my shoe size.
> My father knows what kind of books I read.
>
> My friend knows where I drink.
> My husband knows the colour of my hair.
> My children know my rules.
>
> My dentist knows I need another filling.
> My boss knows I work late.
> My cat knows that I'll share a turkey sandwich.
>
> I know what makes me laugh.
> I laugh at what they don't know.
> They don't know very much about my dentist.
>
> *Sophie Hannah*

3 Check **complex sentences** in the glossary.

Procedure

1 Ask your students to look at the people listed on the blackboard. These are some of the people in a person's life. Ask your students to suggest others and write these in the box. They can also suggest pets and mascots that are important in their lives. List these too in the box:

my cat
my teddy
my pillow
my best friend
my pen friend

2 Ask your students this question.

What do each of these people know about you?

Ask them to think about what special information each person on the list has about them and share this with a neighbour.

3 Ask each learner to draw up their own personal list of 'special people/pets'.

4 For each person/pet on the list, ask them to complete the sentence with one thing he/she knows about them:

My cat knows …
My sister knows …
My best friend knows …

After the clause *My cat knows* the learner can add:

- a noun to finish the sentence (*My cat knows my name.*)
  OR
- a whole phrase (*I talk in my sleep.*)

With less advanced learners you may want to practise just the first pattern:

My mother knows my birthday.
My sister knows my dreams.

With more advanced learners you may want to practise the second pattern:

My cat knows I talk in my sleep.
My sister knows I eat lots of chocolate.

5 Invite your students to share their poems with one another and to read the poems around the walls and compare their ideas.

Variations

A variation that works well is:
My mother doesn't know …
My father doesn't know …

Another is to reverse the sentence:
I know my cat …
I know my mother …
I know my best friend …
I know my sister …

What do you know about them?

I know *my cat purrs in his sleep.*
I know *my mother reads romantic novels.*

4.7 Poems about first days: *Surprised by mashed potato*

Level Intermediate to advanced

Time 25 minutes

Aims To practise and enrich vocabulary for describing feelings.

Procedure

1 Ask your students to think about one of the following situations. Choose the one that best suits their age and situation:

- my first day at school/college/university
- my first day in this country
- my first day leaving my parents
- my first day in a new job
- my first journey to another country

Ask the group to share with you some adjectives to describe what they felt. Some that groups have suggested are in Column A below:

Column A	Column B
Surprised about/by	the number of ...
Disappointed about/by	the smell of ...
Worried about/by	the taste of ...
Amused about/by	the colour of ...
Confused about/by	the shape of ...
Excited about/by	the sound of ...
Delighted about/by	the people: teachers/children/
Pleased about/by	the noises/sounds/words
Disgusted about/by	
Happy about	
Sad about	
Nervous about	
Pleased about	

2 Now explain they are going to say a little more about each of those feelings.

Most of the adjectives can be expanded, using the structure *adjective + about + noun*. Some can also be expanded using the structure *adjective + by + noun*. Write three or four of these on the blackboard.

3 Now ask your students the question:

Surprised by what?
Confused by what?
Excited by what?

Give them one minute to think about this and to share their ideas with a neighbour. Then elicit some ideas to finish each of the phrases on the board.

4   Write their ideas on the blackboard so that each phrase is completed by a noun.

Surprised by school bells
Confused by the teacher
Excited by all the children
Disappointed by the food

5   Ask the class to work in groups of two and three. Ask each group to write lines of their own using one of these alternatives.

- each group member uses the same adjective, so the verse has the pattern

  Surprised by …
  Surprised by …
  Surprised by …

- each group member uses a different adjective, so the verse has the pattern

  Surprised by …
  Confused by …
  Disappointed by …

6   After ten minutes, ask the groups to join up and read their lines to one another.

They could also compare their own lines to the ones below.

First days in England

Surprised by school bells
Surprised by kindness
Surprised by language
Surprised by shyness
Surprised by the number of children
Surprised by bright colour paints
Surprised by feet smell
Surprised by mashed potato

Turkish children in London

Follow-up

Some groups may notice there are adjectives with other patterns:

Interested in
Homesick for
Delighted with

If your class are more advanced, and wish to use these other patterns, suggest that they do so, creating repeated lines as suggested in stage 4 above:

Interested in the strange language
Interested in the strange people
Interested in the strange food

4.8 Mashed sentence poem: *I am fond of bananas*

Level Intermediate to advanced

Time 20 minutes

Aims To experiment with syntax and to look at how word order changes meaning.

Preparation

Prepare each of the words in the sentences below on large pieces of card so you can move them around in different ways. Also prepare a set of five or six empty cards.

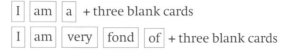

I | am | a + three blank cards

I | am | very | fond | of + three blank cards

Procedure

1 Show the cards with the words, by sticking them on the wall or the blackboard. Ask your students to suggest words for the blank cards in each sentence. Write two or three of their suggestions on the blank cards.

2 Now explain that you are going to move the cards around. Move them at random and ask your class:

Is the sentence still grammatically correct?
What does the sentence mean now?
Which possible changes can I make so the sentence still makes sense?

3 Ask your students to write down as many sentence changes as they can in two minutes. They could also do this in teams of three or four.

4 After two minutes find out which team has the greatest number of possible correct sentences. You could make the following points: Words move about in phrases or chunks rather than on their own.

For example:
- the verb phrase (*I am*)
- the adjectival phrase (*very fond of*)
- the noun phrase (*a poet*)

Encourage your students to notice these chunks and to keep them complete.

For example:
- *I poet very am of fond*

is less interesting and meaningful than
- *Very fond of a poet I am*

5 Now invite your students to write two sentences of their own. They could use the sentence structure you have suggested or another simple one of their own.

6 Invite them to transform the sentences in the same way, writing as many as they can in ten minutes. Then invite groups to share their poems. Here is an example from students in Bedford.

> I have many struggles to learn English.
> It is not so easy.
> I have to learn English.
> To learn English is not many struggles.
> To learn English is not so easy.
> Easy English is not.
> Not English is to learn struggles.
> I have many English struggles.

Variation

Ask your students to exchange nonsense poems with one another and notice which parts make sense and which do not. With a more advanced class, it may be possible to use this as an awareness-raising task and elicit certain interesting rules, such as:

- prepositions need to be next to or near a phrase
- articles need to be next to or near a noun
- verbs and pronouns need to be next to or near one another
- noun phrases can grow and grow with new adjectives introduced
- there is a limit to how big a verb phrase can grow.

Comments

The poem below is an example of the kind of experiment with syntax which your students will try out for themselves during this activity. It is important to present this activity as an experiment in 'nonsense poetry'. If you feel this concept will be simply too confusing for your class, and they will not enjoy the humour and experimentation, wait until they are more confident in the language. This is certainly an activity for students who feel a certain mastery over the sentence!

> I am a poet.
> I am very fond of bananas.
>
> I am bananas.
> I am very fond of a poet.
>
> I am a poet of bananas.
> I am very fond.
>
> A fond poet of 'I am, I am' –
> Very bananas.
>
> Fond of 'Am I bananas?
> Am I?' – a very poet.
>
> Bananas of a poet!
> Am I fond? Am I very?
>
> Poet bananas! I am.
> I am fond of a 'very'.
>
> I am fond of very bananas.
> Am I a poet?
>
> *Wendy Cope*

5
Time poems

This chapter looks at the way we express time in English. The focus is on verb forms and what they tell us about past, present, and future times, and the relationships between them. The poems also try and uncover what we feel about each of these time frames. Present time is not only about where we are physically, but where our thoughts are, how the outside differs from the inside, what we are observing around us.

The past is about history and myth, personal memory, as well as cultural and communal memory. Ancient times are as much a part of the past tense as the events of yesterday are. The past allows us to see patterns, trace change, and tell stories.

The future is the place where our hopes and aspirations belong, as well as resolutions to do better.

This chapter explores the language patterns and the feelings behind each of these time frames.

5.1 Poems about age: *Being young, being old*

Level Lower-intermediate to advanced

Time 20 minutes

Aims To practise the present simple for describing conditions/states of mind.

Preparation

1 Copy the following chart onto the blackboard.

> I'm old enough to ...
> I'm young enough to ...

Procedure

1 Invite your students to think about ways of finishing each of the sentences on the board. Give them a few suggestions of your own to help them. Write their suggestions on the blackboard. The following ideas have been suggested by students:

```
I'm old enough to ...          leave home
I'm young enough to ...        write my memoirs
                               dance
                               stay up all night
                               fail exams
                               stop going to school
                               get a job
                               learn a language
                               go home to my country
                               be a poet
                               have a baby
                               have a boyfriend
                               get married
```

2 When you have written five or six ideas on the blackboard, read them aloud with your class.

3 Now ask your class to work in groups of four or six. Ask each member of the group to write one sentence for *old enough ...* and one sentence for *young enough ...* .

4 When all the sentences have been written, invite the members of each group to listen to one another's lines, and to arrange them in pairs, or verses of four. Encourage them to experiment with the lines to find the most interesting order for them.

5 After ten minutes ask each group to read back their lines to the rest of the class. You may also wish to share with them the following poems.

Eleven Years Old

I'm old enough
to work in the fields,
my grandmother says:
Your limbs are young
and strong,
your mind won't rust,
we need the extra hands
to tend the crop
and feed the goats
and till this ungrateful land,

Dionne Brand, Trinidad

I'm young enough to play in the street.
I'm old enough to write a diary.

I'm young enough to wear jeans
I'm old enough to have long memories

I'm old enough to babysit
I'm young enough to dance all night.

I'm young enough to have many dreams.
I'm old enough to know some are not true.

Workshop ideas

Follow-up

Another variation of this activity is:

I'm too young to …
I'm too old to …

Advanced learners may be interested in the following:

Warning by Jenny Joseph
This poem starts: *When I am old I will wear purple*

'When I'm sixty four' Beatles song, from the album *Sergeant Pepper's Lonely Hearts Club Band.*

Comments

The word that follows this structure is in the **infinitive form with** *to*.

Typical errors are:

missing out the *to* in the infinitive form (*I'm old enough leave home.*)
missing out the verb altogether (*I'm young enough still at school.*)

5.2 Busy activity poems: *Here is a beehive*

Level Lower-intermediate to advanced

Time 20 minutes

Aims To practise the *-ing* form. To enrich vocabulary by collecting as many verbs as possible to describe actions.

Preparation

1 Your class will work in groups of three and four. Decide how many groups you will need and prepare a card for each one, with one of the topics below listed on each card. You could add topics of your own which your students might enjoy and which practise the *-ing* form.

traffic on a busy road
people in the rush hour in a big city
animals: *cats, dogs, fish, horses*
insects: *bees, mosquitoes, flies, spiders*

2 Prepare the poem below to share with your class, either by reading aloud or to display.

> sweating sighing
> struggling
> giving up
> sweating sighing
> giving up
> drinking coffee
> drinking coffee
> failing
> dreaming
> passing
> dreaming
> giving up
> trying again
> trying again

Class poem: Bedford language learners

Procedure

1 Share the poem with your class. Ask your students to guess what the poem is about.
Possible answers are: passing an exam, a difficult task.

2 Ask your students to notice how many *-ing* words there are in the poem.
Can you suggest more -ing words to add to the list?

Here are some ideas suggested by students:

crying
studying, sleeping,
writing, scratching

3 Now divide your class into groups of two or three. Give each group a label with a different topic and ask them to write as many *-ing* words as they can in ten minutes. The list on the next page may be helpful.

4 After ten minutes, ask the groups to join with one another and read their lists without a title. See if the groups can guess each other's titles.

5 This poem works well read aloud as a 'cascade'. This means:

each student or group has a few *-ing* words to read aloud
before they have finished, the next group starts reading their words
before they have finished, the next group starts
and so on, so the voices overlap with one another.

> sweating sighing
> struggling
> giving up
> sweating sighing

Topics:	-*ing* words
traffic on a busy road	puffing, fuming, driving, screeching, turning, braking, hooting, honking
animals: cats, dogs, fish, horses	creeping, running, licking, eating, jumping, sleeping, fighting, playing
insects: bees, mosquitoes, flies, spiders	buzzing, scratching, floating, sucking, crawling, flying, eating, biting
people in the rush hour in a big city	running, pushing, shoving, reading, chewing, listening to headphones, talking on the mobile

Follow-up

Advanced classes may enjoy the poem below as an example of an -*ing* poem.

Beehive

Here is a beehive.
Here is activity of a bee hive.

Grooming cleaning tending feeding fanning breathing
resting brushing
against bumping secreting wax clustering guarding
checking
Shivering wing-muscles chewing nudging constructing
–unloading
storing drumming probing regurgitating food-exchanging
hovering asking defending
tasting navigating-by-the-sun buzzing listening resonating
vibrating balancing
carrying disseminating pollinating wiping licking
wandering patroling
rubbing against touching stumbling dropping attending
repairing reverberating

Jean Symons from *Hiding in Chips*

Comments

The main area of accuracy in this activity is forming the -*ing* words correctly. Typical errors are:

- not doubling the final letter (*stoping*, instead of *stopping*).
- not dropping the final -*e* before adding -*ing* (*caveing*, instead of *caving*).

5.3 Ancient monuments speak: *Slaves and princes*

Level Lower-intermediate to advanced

Time 20 minutes

Aims To practise the present perfect as a way of describing memories.

Preparation

If you can, bring to this class pictures of famous buildings, statues, landscapes, bridges, and monuments which your class will know, and display these on your classroom walls.

Procedure

1 Ask your students to look at the picture of the place you have chosen or use the picture at the beginning of this activity. Explain you are going to think about what this place:

has seen
has heard

Invite suggestions and write these up on the blackboard, adapting students' suggestions to complete the sentences:

You have heard …
You have seen …
You have known …

There are some suggestions in Column B below. If your students 'dry up' after two or three suggestions, introduce another place to them from the list.

A Places	B you have seen/heard/known
the Taj Mahal *Pyramids* *the River Nile* *Eiffel Tower* *Statue of Liberty* *the Galapagos* *the North Pole* *Sahara Desert* *the Forbidden City, Beijing* *volcanos: Popocatépetl* *(Mexico),* *Stromboli (Italy)*	*the sadness of a king* *the death of a king* *camels in the desert* *people in boats* *wonderful animals* *white bears* *large birds* *thousands of languages* *thousands of people* *war, bombs* *presidents, princes, kings* *big statues, temples, palaces* *stone, marble* *hot oven of fire*

2 Now divide the class into groups of two and three. Give each group a picture or the name of a place. There are some suggestions in Column A above.

3 Ask the groups to work for ten minutes, writing as many examples as they can to finish the sentences: *You have heard/seen/known …*

4 After ten minutes, invite them to join another group and read their lines to one another. They could also guess the title of each other's poems.

The following poems below could also be used as examples.

The Pyramids

I have seen camels
and then cars
I have seen slaves
and then princes
I have seen stone
and then marble
I have seen life
and then death

Eiffel Tower

You have heard bombs falling
You have seen Presidents walking
You have seen people travelling by horse
and then by car
You have heard people speaking in a thousand languages
You have seen a million sunsets

Taj Mahal

You have seen the sadness of a king
You have seen the death of a queen
You have seen marble, gold and pearl
You have seen reflections in the water
You have seen buffalo in the river
You have seen saris with a thousand colours like butterflies

Language learners: Totnes, Oxford, and Plymouth

Comments

Make sure that a noun follows the present perfect structure (*camels, white bears, visitors*).

If your students want to give more information, they will need to add an *-ing* form (*camels walking, visitors talking, buffalos washing*).

It is also possible to add the information without an *-ing* (*You have seen camels walk/You have seen visitors talk.*)

Accept both possibilities as correct.

5.4 Memory poems: *Now I'm a poet*

Level Lower-intermediate and intermediate

Time 20 minutes

Aims To describe changes between the present and the past.
To practise *used to* for past memories.

Procedure

1 Ask students to think about one friend or relation they like very much. Ask them to share with the class some of the names or descriptions of these people.

2 Invite students to remember their friend or relation – any traditions they had together, their earlier meetings and times together, ways the friendship has changed. Ask students to share their ideas with a neighbour.

3 After a few minutes, invite the students to suggest ways of finishing the sentences.

   a *We used to …*
   b *but now we …*
   c *You used to …*
   d *but now you …*

Write their ideas on the blackboard as an example.

| We used to | talk on the telephone | but now we write emails. |
| You used to | be shy | but now you talk all the time. |

4 Now give the student ten minutes to write down pairs of sentences like these:

We used to …
but now we …

You used to …
but now you …

The phrases below may be helpful.

| We used to
But now we | talk
walk
eat ice-creams
walk along the beach
talk on the phone
write long letters
buy presents
sit in cafés
laugh
tell jokes |
| You used to be
But now you are | shy
sad
kind
funny
happy |

5   After ten minutes, ask students to share their poems in a small group or with their neighbour. Below is an example you may wish to share.

> We used to walk alone, along the beach
> But now we walk along the wind
> We used to sing songs in the choir
> But now we sing on the clouds
> We used to go through the trees
> But now we are walking through the
> Brightness
>
> *Creative English class, Plymouth*

Variation

An interesting variation of this activity is

I used to be ...
but now I am ...

Here is an example:

> I used to be shy
> but now I am not
> I used to be disloyal
> but now I've changed
> I used to not know myself
> but now I know who I am
> I used to dislike poetry
> but now I've become a poet
> I used to be a person
> And I still am.
>
> *Miranda Loizidou: Creative English class, Plymouth*

Comments

Focus on the structure *used to*. Some typical errors in this structure are:

- missing out the *to* (*I used go*)
- putting the verb in the wrong form (*I used to going*).

5.5 Inner and outer poems: *Not climbing but falling*

Level   Lower-intermediate to upper-intermediate

Time   20 minutes

Aims   To describe the difference between outside appearance and inner feelings. To practise the structure *was ... -ing* (the past continuous).

Procedure

1   Ask students to think about a time when they said goodbye to a close friend or relation. Where were they?

2 Ask them to choose/remember the time of day when this happened and write one of the times on the blackboard.

At 8.00 p.m.

3 Invite your students to help you build an *-ing* sentence on the board, such as:

I was saying goodbye at the airport/station/bus station

What were you THINKING when you said goodbye?
What were you FEELING?
What were you SEEING?
On the outside you were saying goodbye, but what were you doing on the inside? in your thoughts?

Elicit ideas from the class and add these to the blackboard, using the same structure.

4 Now give the students one minute to write down four sentences of their own, like the ones on the blackboard. They can choose sentences already on the board or write new ones of their own.

I was saying goodbye
I was looking at the clock
I was feeling sad
I was dreaming about our next meeting
I was holding an umbrella

---

5 Tell students they are now going to change their sentences. For each sentence, they are going to add: *not… but*

Make these changes with the class sentences on the board, using the student's suggestions. For example…

I was not saying goodbye, but saying hello
I was not looking at the clock, but feeling sad

The verbs in the box below may be helpful. They are organized in groups of opposites, which will help your students to write their poems.

	not	but
I was You were We were	talking saying hello smiling laughing singing swimming climbing sleeping	thinking saying goodbye frowning crying praying drowning falling dreaming

6   Give students five minutes to write their own personal poems. Each verse will have the same pattern:

I was not … ing   but … ing

They can also vary these sentences if they wish to.

7   When they have finished, ask students to share their poems in a small group or with their neighbour.

Variations

1   Other topics that work well are:

when I first came to this country OR
when I first left home

Below is an example from Turkish children in central London.

When I came to this country

I was not laughing but crying
I was not crying but hoping
I was not hoping but already living
I was not climbing but falling
I was not falling but climbing

Turkish primary school children, Haringey, London

2   More advanced learners may also be interested in reading the poem below and discussing:

What is happening on the outside?
What is happening on the inside?

Not Waving, But Drowning

Nobody heard him, the dead man,
But still he lay moaning:
I was much further out than you thought
And not waving but drowning

Poor chap, he always loved larking
And now he's dead
It must have been too cold for him his heart gave way,
They said.

Oh no, no,no, it was too cold always
(Still the dead one lay moaning)
I was much too far out all my life
And not waving but drowning.

Stevie Smith

Comments

The *I was* does not need to be repeated in both parts of the sentence. The *I was* is understood in the second part. It is actually there 'silently'. This is called ellipsis.

5.6 Talking about the past: *I remember the sight of nothing*

Level Elementary to upper-intermediate

Time 20 minutes

Aims To practise different patterns for *I remember* and to recall childhood memories.

Procedure

1 Ask your students to think about one of the following situations. Choose one you think will be relevant to your students:

My first day at school
The first day I left home (to go to college, marry, work, or go overseas)
My first day in this country
My first holiday without my parents

2 Ask your students to think hard about the situation, then to write down five sentences, each beginning:

I remember ...
If your students need some help at this stage, ask them to write

I remember + a smell
*   a sound*
*   a sight*
*   a taste*
*   a person*

3 After five minutes ask the students to share their sentences with others in their group.

4 You could now ask the students to make patterns of *I remember* lines:

Less advanced learners could use patterns 1, 2, and 3.
More advanced learners could use patterns 4 and 5.

Pattern 1 five lines with *I remember* + a person or an object
Pattern 2 five lines with *I remember* + an -*ing* verb
          (*I remember feeling/seeing/thinking/hearing*)
Pattern 3 five lines with *I remember* + a smell, sight, or a sound
Pattern 4 five lines with *I remember* + a verb in the simple past
          (*I remember I felt sad*)
Pattern 5 five lines with *I remember* + *that* + a verb in the simple past
          (*I remember that I was worried*)

5 Invite your students to share and compare their memories.

The following poems can also be shared. More advanced learners could read these and notice which *I remember* patterns are being used. There are some definite articles missed out by the students in poem 1. You might want your group to spot these, correct them, and decide which version they prefer.

First day at school

I remember football
I remember teacher
I remember my father
I remember sumo
I remember children
I remember feeling excited
I remember school bus
I remember friend
I remember climbing frame
I remember my mother

Omani and Japanese learners, Plymouth

I remember the sight of nothing
I remember the smell of nothing
I remember the taste of nothing
I remember the sound of nothing

There were many children
There were many teachers
There were many textbooks

I ate school lunch

There was a lot of lunch

But

I remember the sight of nothing
I remember the smell of nothing
I remember the taste of nothing
I remember the sound of nothing

Junko Hozu: Japanese student, Plymouth

5.7 Feelings: *If love was a sweet*

Level Lower-intermediate to upper-intermediate

Time 20 minutes

Aims To practise the conditional structure *If I was … I would*. To compare abstract feelings and concrete objects.

Procedure

1 Write the following half sentence on the board:

> If love was …

Invite students to complete the clause with words of their own. Write up their words on the blackboard. You can use some of the suggestions in the box below if the students need help.

If	love friendship happiness kindness	was	a trumpet a star a flower a cloud a tree a sweet

2 Ask students to choose just one of the completed clauses. This is going to be the first line of the class poem. For example, *If love was a trumpet.*

They are now going to write the second line:

I'd …

Invite them to finish that sentence too. *What would you do with a trumpet?*

blow it
play it
shout it out

They have now written the first verse of a poem:

If love was a trumpet
I'd shout it out

3 Give students five minutes to write as many verses of the poem as they like. Each verse will have two lines and include a new description of love.

4 If students enjoy this, they can also change *love* to another word. There are some suggestions in the list above.

5 They can also add other lines using more ideas of their own:

But love isn't a …
It's a …

You could also share with them the examples below.

If love was a sweet
I'd gather candies
And make a fleet

If love was a sweet
I'd sprinkle love
Using a peaceful fleet

If love was a sweet
I'd gather candies
And make a fleet

Junko: Japanese student

If friendship was a bottle of wine
    It would smell good
If friendship was a drum
    It would feel powerful
If friendship was a poem
    It would read sensitively
If friendship was a sweet
    It would taste nice.

Alice: Japanese student

If love was jazz,
I'd be dazzled
By its razzamatazz.

If love was a sax
I'd melt in its brassy flame
Like wax.

If love was a guitar,
I'd pluck its six strings,
Eight to a bar.

If love was a trombone,
I'd feel its slow
Slide, right down my backbone.

If love was a drum,
I'd be caught in its snare,
Kept under its thumb.

If love was a trumpet
I'd blow it.

If love was jazz,
I'd sing its praises,
Like Larkin has.

But love isn't jazz.
It's an organ recital.
Eminently worthy,
Not nearly as vital.

If love was jazz,
I'd always want more.
I'd be a regular
On that smoky dance-floor.

Linda France

Variations

An interesting variation is to reverse the comparison. Compare a real thing with an abstract feeling:

If my home were love, I would…
If books were wisdom, I would…

Follow-up

Advanced learners may like to collect, or look at, quotations and idioms which use this kind of comparison. For example,

If music be the food of love, play on! (from Shakespeare's *Twelfth Night*)

Comments

Make sure your students do not confuse the *if* clause, and the second clause. Typical errors are:

writing the *would* in both clauses (*If love would be jazz, I would fly …*)
writing the *would* in neither clause (*If love was jazz, I flew …*)

6

Modal verb poems

This chapter explores the many meanings conveyed through modal verbs *can, may, might, should, ought*. Each poem practises the patterns and explores a specific modal usage and meaning.

Modals have the advantage of a very simple form. They do not change with different pronouns and with few exceptions they can be used in only one tense and yet modals convey a subtle variety of meanings – shades of obligation, from gentle suggestion to compulsion, shades of sureness from vague speculation to absolute certainty.

The activities in this chapter will work with these subtleties.

Activity 6.1 looks at how modals help us to guess with varying degrees of certainty.

Activity 6.2 looks at how modals help us to dream, speculate, and build utopias.

Activity 6.3 looks at how we use modals to discuss our values.

Activity 6.4 looks at how we use modals to give advice and try and guide the actions of others.

Activity 6.5 sets up a poetry market using modals to buy and sell poems.

Activity 6.6 looks at how we use modals to formulate rules. In this case, the focus is on personal rules, and the laws of a new community that your students will invent.

6.1 Guessing poems: *A note folded inside a diary*

Level Elementary to advanced

Time 20 minutes

Aims To practise modals used for making guesses and predictions.

Materials

Bring to the classroom a small container of some kind, such as

a wooden box
a small jewellery box
a small pot with a lid

Each student in the class will need a small piece of paper.

Procedure

1 Show your class the box or object you have brought to class. Explain: *Inside the box is the thing you most want. You may not be able to see or touch this thing.* Ask the class to imagine what it could be, using one or more of the structures below.

It could be …
It might be …
It may be …
Maybe it is …
Possibly it is …

The guesses can be objects or abstract ideas depending on the level and abilities of your class.

The poem below includes guesses made by other learners which you could share.

What's in the box?

it could be a wish
it could be a penny in a pond
it could be a shadow against the wall
it might be a wedding ring
it might be a summer memory
it might be a toy
it could be a ticket to China

Maybe it's something you can write with
or something you can draw with
Maybe it's something you can read
or a poem you can write
or a flute you can play
or a song you can sing.
Maybe it's a dream you once had
or a note folded inside a diary.

International teachers' workshop in Exeter

2 Now ask your students to imagine putting a small gift into the box . It could be an idea, a thought, a memory, or an object. The gift can be for a friend, lover, relation, for people in the future. They should write this down on a small piece of paper, fold it up, and hide it.

3 Now ask them to work with a partner. Each partner should guess what their neighbour has put into the box. They should write at least four sentences, like the ones in the poem, but using new words of their own.

What is your gift?
It might be a thought about your country.
It might be a stone from your country.
It might be a smile.

4 After ten minutes invite the partners to read their 'guessing poems' to one another. When they have finished, open up the small piece of paper and see if their partners have guessed correctly.

The students could share with you at the end of the class what gifts they put in the box and why.

Variation

A variation of this activity for elementary learners leads to a list poem.

Ask your students to write down the gift they will put in the box and the wish they will put in the box. In groups of four and five, ask the students to draw up a list of all their wishes and gifts. If they need to, they could write the words in the mother tongue, and check with you or the dictionary for a translation.

Here is one example from a class.

> Wishes
> a memory
> a thought of my country
> a motorbike
> a telephone
>
> Gifts
> a football
> a song
> a lump of sugar
> a stone
> a photograph

Activity 8.3 gives you more ideas about list poems.

Comments

Your students may be interested to know the difference between each of the modals listed on the blackboard.

You could discuss degrees of certainty with them and draw a line plotting each of the modals.

absolutely sure		not sure at all
it must be	it could be	it might be

There is no single correct position on the line for each modal. It is the discussion which matters.

6.2 Ideal world poems: *A place with no schools*

Level Intermediate to advanced

Time 20 minutes

Aims To practise levels of certainty using *must* and *may*. To practise clauses with relative pronouns.

Preparation

1 Write the sentence below on the board:
There must be more than this.

2 Check **relative pronouns** in the glossary.

Procedure

1 Ask your students to think about the sentence on the board.
They can interpret the sentence in any way they like. It could lead them to think about life, future travels and studies, afterlife, religion and beliefs. Or they could think about what there is outside the class, the school, and the language lesson where they are sitting now.

2 When they have had time to think and talk about the sentence, invite them to suggest what the *more* could be, by adding further sentences beginning:
There must be ....

Here are some sentences which other classes have suggested.

There must be better weather somewhere
There must be a place with all same language *
There must be a place with no schools
There must be somewhere with no war

* Take care not to offer this as a grammatical example. It is learner language – not grammatically correct, but poetic!

3 Now ask the class to work in groups of three or four. Ask each member of the group to take one of the four patterns below.
There must be a place where …
There must be a time when …
There must be someone who …
There must be a reason why …

and write one sentence in their pattern.

4 When they are ready, ask them to share their lines to form a verse of the poem.

Follow-up

The different lines the groups have written can be combined in several ways to form class poems.

Each group poem can form one verse, OR all the students who wrote the same patterns could work together and form verses that repeat the pattern. For example:

There must be a place where people have what they want.
There must be a place where people have enough to eat.
There must be a place where people have enough to drink.

More advanced learners might enjoy the poem below. Invite them to notice the rhyme words in the poem. Encourage them to return to their own verses and make two lines in each verse rhyme with one another.

> There must be some light somewhere
> There must be a true other,
> There must be more than despair,
> There must be more my brother.
>
> There must be so much unsaid
> There must be an informant,
> There must be some truth ahead,
> There must be a judgement.
>
> *Benjamin Zephaniah*

Comments

After each of the phrases at Stage 3 above, the students must write a complete sentence, with a subject and a verb. Typical errors are:

- to miss out part of the complete sentence (*There must be a place where people free.* – the verb is missing).
- to miss out the 'linking' word or relative pronoun who, where, why (*There must be a time people happy.* – 'when' is missing).

6.3 Values poem: *You can't cuddle money*

Level Lower-intermediate to upper-intermediate

Time 20 minutes

Aims To practise and revise *can* for ability. To think about personal values and attitudes to concepts such as fame, money, power, fashion.

Procedure

1 Write the following sentence on the board and ask your class to look at it carefully.

You can't	eat	money

Is the sentence true or not true?

Do you agree with the sentence?
What do you think it really means? Do you think anyone really believes you can eat money? What DO people really believe?

2   Ask the class to suggest other things which money can't do. Write their ideas on the board.

Below are some ideas you could use to help your students.

A	B	C
You can't	eat drink write letters to cuddle talk to wrap presents with tell your secrets to borrow clothes from bandage a finger with	money

3   After five minutes ask the class to read out the sentences they have written. You could orchestrate this with each row of students/group of students reading one sentence each.

4   If the students have enjoyed this, add the following extra words to Column C.

> *fame*
> *power*
> *glamour*
> *prizes*
> *fast cars*
> *computer games*
> *expensive clothes*

5   Ask students to work in groups of two or three. They should choose a new word from Column C and in their group write at least five sentences beginning *You can't … .*

6   After ten minutes ask groups to read their sentences to each other.

Follow-up

Some students may enjoy reading and discussing the following poem by James Berry.

What is he telling us about money?

How do his ideas compare to yours?

Why do you think he uses such strong images? What is he telling us in these images?

Fantasy of an African Boy

Such a peculiar lot
we are, we people
without money, in daylong
yearlong sunlight, knowing
money is somewhere, somewhere.

And we can't eat it.

We can't drink it up.

We can't read money for books.

We can't use money to bandage
sores, can't pound it
to powder for sick eyes
and sick bellies. Yet without
it, flesh melts from our bones.

James Berry

Comments

The main structure to check in your students' writing is:

You can't + infinitive without 'to'

Typical errors are:

Writing two negatives (*You can't not …*)
Writing the verb in the *to be* form (infinitive) (*You can't to do …*)

Check **root** and **infinitive** in the glossary if these are unclear.

6.4 Giving advice: *If you want to be free*

Level   **Lower-intermediate to advanced**

Time   **20 minutes**

Aims   **To practise modals for giving advice.**

Procedure

1   Write the following incomplete sentence on the board and ask your students to suggest adjectives to complete the first half of the sentence. Write their ideas on the board.

> If you want to be _____ you should _____

Here are some ideas suggested by classes:

free, clever, happy, good, rich, kind, famous

2   Ask your students to choose one of the adjectives you have written on the board and to suggest advice for achieving this using any of the structures for giving advice in Column A on the next page. Select these according to the level of your class. There are suggestions for advice in Column B.

> *If you want to be* _____
>
> | A | B |
> |---|---|
> | you should | *work hard* |
> | you need to | *buy a big car* |
> | you have to | *speak quietly* |
> | you ought to | *make friends with your boss* |
> | it would be a good idea to | *live with a cat* |
> | | *lose weight* |
> | | *win a big prize* |

3 Now divide the class into groups of two and three. Ask each group to choose another adjective and to write advice poems of their own. Less advanced learners could write two-line verses. Each pair of lines would use a different adjective.

Your students may enjoy the following poem as an example.

> If you want to be happy
> you should speak quietly
> you should sing and not shout
> you should live with a cat
> you should put the TV in a sack
> you should grow a flower
>
> If you want to be free
> you should not carry anger
> you should not frighten anyone
> you should not show your open hand
>
> *Creative English class: Plymouth*

6.5 Poetry market: *Poems for sale!*

Level Intermediate to upper-intermediate

Time 25 minutes

Aims To practise modals for making recommendations and persuading.

Materials

- The picture at the beginning of this activity
- The three poems as examples

Preparation

The poems below could be written on large labels, like signs in a market, and displayed around the room. You could add price tags for more authenticity.

Buy my beautiful poem!

You really should hear its fine words
You really should learn its wise words.

Buy my beautiful poem!
It will tell you about the world.
It will teach you to think well.

Buy my beautiful poem!
It can sing!
It can play the banjo!

> **Poem for free!**
>
> Come and hear my poem!
> You can hear my poem for free!
>
> This poem can tell your dreams.
> This poem can write your thoughts.
> This poem can tell stories.
> This poem can stay awake all night.
> This poem can make lunch for you!
>
> This poem can do all this
> and for free!

> Can a poem listen to your problems? Yes!
> Can a poem give you advice? Yes!
> Can a poem last a lifetime? Yes!
> Can a poem travel with you everywhere? Yes!
> Can a poem make you laugh? Yes!
> Can a poem sleep under your pillow? Yes!
> Can a poem visit you unexpectedly? Yes!
> Can I buy a poem with wind and air? Yes!

Author's scripts for workshop, Switzerland

Procedure

1 Ask your students to look at the picture.

Where is this place? (a market)
Is it a normal market? What are people selling?
What do you think the people at the stalls are shouting?

Invite them to look at the poems displayed around the room.

Who is saying these words?
How would they be spoken?

2 Explain you are going to set up a poetry market. In the poetry market people sell their poems. Each student (or pair of students) is going to write a poem to sell at the market. The poem can start:

Buy my poem!

Then it will do one or more of these things:

- explain why it is so special
- explain why someone should buy it
- explain what the buyer can do with it

3 Elicit some ideas on the blackboard. The suggestions below were made by students:

This poem	can will	paint pictures sing dance make you laugh tell stories stay up all night keep you awake be funny be sad make you cry play the guitar
This poem	is	home-made delightful
You	really should ought to must	read it try it out listen to it learn from it learn the words dance to it write your own buy it

4 Now ask the class to work in pairs or groups to write their own poem. The structures above are suggested patterns the students can use. Each poem should be four or five lines long.

They can be as surprising or unusual as the students want. Their poems can dance, sing, knit, and make lunch if they wish!

5 After ten minutes invite each group to read their poem aloud and also to make a note of the poem they would like to buy.

6 Share choices at the end of the lesson. Which poem was the most popular? How much should it cost?

Variations

Variations which work well include:

- selling an invention
- selling a wonder-medicine or wonder-food.

6.6 New Community Ten Commandments: *Be kind when you can*

Level Lower-intermediate to advanced

Time 25 minutes

Aims To practise modals for giving rules and regulations.

Procedure

1 Ask your students to think about the 'rules' or commandments they were taught from childhood. Some of these rules may come from their parents, some from school, some from scriptures. Ask your students to share some of these rules with a neighbour.

You must not talk and eat.
You must not lie to people.
You must not chew gum in the house.
You must not wear shoes in the house.

2 Write some of their ideas on the blackboard. It might be interesting to see whether your students were taught the same things or whether different rules were remembered. This will depend on whether your class all belongs to the same cultural or ethnic group, or whether they are from many different backgrounds.

3 Now divide the class into groups of four or five. Explain that each group is setting up a new community and they must agree on ten laws or commandments for the community.

The group must agree on which ten rules are the best and draw up a list. The structures below can be used as the pattern for their rules.

New Community Commandments	
You shall	You shall not
You must	You must not

Below are examples from Czech teachers.

You must be good when you can
You must be kind when you can
You must do your best when you can't
and not be bad-tempered
You must not lie to friends.
You must be kind to friends and remember their birthdays.

You shall study hard.
You shall not chew gum indoors.
You shall be nice to your parents.
You shall wash up after all meals.
You shall say thank you when parents give you money.
You shall send postcards from holidays.

You must try to be happy.
You must try and make things good.

Workshop for Czech literature teachers

4 After 15 minutes ask the groups to read out and compare their lists. Were there any rules which were repeated? Which community seems to have the best set of rules? Why?

Follow-up

An interesting follow-up is for each group to give their community a name.

Comments

Shall has several meanings. In this exercise it is a modal verb, meaning: *It is a rule, It is compulsory, You are required to …* , and is often used with the pronoun *you*.

Take care that the verb that follows is in the root form with or without *to* as necessary. Typical errors are:

You must not to smoke.

Another typical error is a double negative or incorrect use of the apostrophe:

You mustn't not smoke.
You must'nt smoke.

7

Language function poems

Functions are a way of describing language according to the jobs they do in the real world. 'Present perfect' may tell us about form, but as a title it gives us very little information about the work it does in the world and what we can do with it. Descriptions such as: asking for directions, expressing preferences, inviting, celebrating, complaining, and giving advice, give much clearer information about where the language fits in real-life interaction. We know that inviting will involve an event of some kind – perhaps a party, or a ceremony, or a performance at the theatre. We know that asking directions may be on a street or on a mountain path, and that a journey is involved.

For these reasons, functions tell instant stories. We can guess the relationships of the people speaking. We can guess where they might be and what the situation might be.

The activities in this chapter work with these expectations, but they also stretch the possibilities of what a language function can do. With a few interesting changes, these patterns can start to say a great deal more than they appear to at first and can turn familiar forms into messages which are both musical and surprising.

7.1 Poems about finding the way: *On the corner of night and dreams*

Level Intermediate to advanced

Time 20 minutes

Aims To revise the language of asking and giving directions.

Preparation

Write the following phrases on the board or on a wall display.

Could you tell me the way to ...
Do you know where ... is?
Which way is it to ...?

It's straight on.
You have to turn left.
                              right.
Keep going until you reach ...
It's on the corner of ...
It's just next to ...
It's behind ...
It's opposite ...

Procedure

1 Ask students to look at the phrases in the box above. Ask them:

When would you say these things?
What words would go in the spaces?

The students might suggest answers, such as: *the bank, the post office, the station, the hotel, the shops, the library, the school, the youth hostel.*

2 Now tell the students that these are no ordinary directions. Choose one of the words in Column B below and write this up on the board.

Could you tell me the way to happiness?

Column A	Column B
Could you tell me the way to	*happiness?* *my future?* *my childhood?* *success?* *fame?* *wealth?* *the rainbow?* *sleep?* *friendship?* *adulthood?*

3 If you were directing someone, not to the station but to this other place, where would you tell them to go? Elicit some ideas and examples from the group and write their ideas on the board.

You start at childhood and go straight on until you come to your best friend's house.

4 Now write on the board the other words in column B. Ask students to work in groups of two and three. Each group must choose one of the words and together write the directions to that place.

Less advanced learners may prefer everyday directions, such as: *Start at the bank and keep straight on.*

More advanced learners may want to try the more difficult symbolic language.

5 After ten minutes ask students to share their directions with another group. They could also compare their ideas with the following poems.

> *Can you tell me the way to happiness?*
> It's first on the left then straight ahead.
> Then you come to two ways and you must choose.
> Go left or right?
> Do not listen to your friend.
> Do not listen to your teachers.
> Do not listen to your parents,
> Choose the way you like best.
> That is the way to happiness.

> *Could you tell me the way to sleep?*
> Keep going until you reach the night.
> It's on the corner of night and dreams.
> Wait on the corner a while.
> Sleep will come and find you.

> *Workshop poems from Swedish, Swiss, Indian, and Malaysian teachers*

Comments

Choose the phrases you would like your students to practise and produce correctly. Focus just on these when you are correcting their work and allow other kinds of errors (or report back on these in another lesson).

Typical errors in the use of prepositions are:

It's next of the … , It's behind of the …

Some of your students may use phrases rather than whole sentences:

Behind the …
In front of …

7.2 Poems about getting rid of unwanted clutter: *The reject shop*

Level Intermediate to advanced

Time 20 minutes

Aims To practise the language of complaints.

Materials

The picture at the beginning of this activity.

Procedure

1 Ask your students to look at the picture.

   • *What are all the objects in the picture?*
   • *Where are they all? What are they doing there?*
   • *Do you have a room like this at home?*
   • *If the picture was called* Inside my mind *– what would it mean?*
   • *If someone were to draw the inside of your mind, what would it look like?*

2 Explain that this room is a reject shop – a place where you return products that you don't like any more, or which are damaged.

   What would you send to the reject shop?

   The students' suggestions will probably be household words, such as: *coat, shoes, T-shirt, TV, computer, bicycle, motorbike, washing machine.*

3   Explain the students are not going to return a product from a shop, but something in their lives they don't want any more.

It could be an object that they don't need or use any more, or it could be a feeling or a characteristic they have which is unhelpful or uncomfortable.

Ask the students to think about what they would choose to send to the reject shop, and then tell a partner.

4   Elicit some of their rejects and write these on the blackboard. Examples suggested by classes have included:

Objects
old violin case with no violin inside
letters from ex-boyfriend/ex-girlfriend
clothes which no longer fit
piles of old newspapers
piles of past greetings cards
out-of-date computer equipment
single earrings (the other half has been lost)

Feelings
shyness
laziness
being tired
some memories
jealousy

5   Now ask your students to try and finish the following sentences:
I would like to return shyness because …
it doesn't …
it no longer …
… is wrong
my … doesn't like it
it's too …

Here is an example poem:

> I would like to return shyness because
> It no longer fits
> It doesn't wash well.
> It doesn't feel nice.

6   Divide your class into groups of two or three, and ask each group to choose a new item, and write a poem of their own.

Each poem should explain what item is to be returned (*I am returning …*) and give three or four reasons why the item is no longer wanted.

Reassure your less advanced learners that the poem works very well with abstract ideas (*shyness, laziness*) being described just as if they are a pair of shoes or an old teddy bear.

The ideas and structures below may help them.

I am returning it, because	it's too	big small short long
	the colour the material the design the quality the pattern	is wrong
	it doesn't	wash well fit look nice feel nice match my other one
	my wife my husband my boyfriend my doctor	doesn't like it
	it is no longer	suitable useful required

7   After ten minutes, ask students to share with the class some of the items being rejected and some of the reasons. Invite the students to read their poems aloud.

Follow-up

If more than one student has chosen the same reject item, they could team together and create a poem with two verses.

You could also team together:

- all the students describing household items
- all the students describing difficult feelings
- all the students describing childhood objects or memories.

Each group could then create a long poem, with each student contributing one verse.

Comments

A noun is needed after these phrases.

I am no longer happy with …
I would like to return …

If your students would like to describe feelings and ideas, they need to turn them into nouns (*shy: shyness, lazy: laziness*). They could also use the structure *being* + adjective.

Both the following sentences are possible:

I am no longer happy with being shy/lazy/tired/sad/lonely
I would like to return shyness/laziness/sadness/loneliness

A typical error is to end the sentences with an adjective:

I am no longer happy with shy.

The idea for this poem occurred when I filled out a form, returning a pair of white running shoes to a mail order company. In the same week, I was made redundant from my teaching job after seven years, and began to identify with the poor pair of shoes I had recently returned.

The Reject Shop

I am returning the enclosed.
It was too long
too short
too big
too small
too tight
too loose
the wrong colour/shape/size/cut/texture/fabric/fit
disliked by my lover/daughter/neighbour/dean/doctor/dog
/dentist/psychic counsellor.
I ordered
two by mistake
one by mistake
eleven by mistake
ten by mistake.
It was used
soiled
surplus to requirements
unsatisfactory
no longer required
redundant.
The garment is
reusable
recyclable
unusable
reducible
collapsible
removable.
Please dispose of
quietly
after use

Jane Spiro

7.3 Fairy-tale advice column: *Glass shoes*

Level Lower-intermediate to upper-intermediate

Time 20 minutes

Aims To practise patterns for giving advice.

Procedure

1 Choose one of the situations from the list below, taken from traditional fairy tales and folk tales, and copy it on to the blackboard. You could also use other fairy-tale situations, which you think your students will recognize.

> • You have sent your little sister/brother through the forest to deliver a basket of cherries (Little Red Riding Hood).
> • Your friend tells you she has discovered an empty house and would like to return there with you (Goldilocks and the Three Bears).
> • Your beautiful friend has to go and live in a house with a hideously ugly but likeable monster (Beauty and the Beast).
> • Your best friend has to clean for her two nasty sisters night and day, but longs to go to the Prince's party (Cinderella).

2 Invite your students to think about the character's main problem and the concerns they would have if this were a friend, brother, or sister.

What would they feel sending Red Riding Hood out through the forest?
What would they feel watching their friend Cinderella scrubbing floors night and day?

3 Explain you are going to give this main character some advice to help them in their situation. The advice could begin with the phrases suggested in the picture above:

Don't forget to ...
Remember to ...
Try to ...

or with any of the structures below.

	Don't let ...
	Don't forget to ...
Remember to ...	Remember not to ...
Try to ...	Try not to ...
You should ...	You shouldn't ...
You must ...	You mustn't ...
You ought to ...	You ought not to ...

Ask them to make suggestions and write their ideas on the blackboard. For example:

Cinderella

Don't be sad.
Don't show what you think.
You will go to the party in glass shoes.
Just wait.

Little Red Riding Hood

Take care.
Walk straight on.
Talk to nobody
even if they seem friendly.
Do not share the cherries
even with the birds.
Walk fast so you always have light
and follow where the sun is.

Workshop poems

4 Now give your class other situations to think about. Ask them to choose one of these or another of their own choice and write an advice poem in the same way, with at least five or six short pieces of advice for their character.

5 After 15 minutes ask them to read their poem to a partner. See if the partner can guess the situation they are describing.

Variation

For students who may find fairy-tale characters 'silly', you can use real situations instead. Here are some examples:

Your little sister/brother:

- is going on holiday without the family for the first time
- is travelling to the big city for the first time
- is walking through a big forest on his/her own
- is travelling by plane for the first time
- is starting school or college for the first time

You could also elicit from your class real situations in which they were called upon to give advice and write these on the board.

The poem below would be an interesting one as a model of general advice to someone starting out in life.

> Walk well
> > Walk well
> Don't let thorns run in you
> Or let a cow butt you.
> Don't let a dog bite you
> Or hunger catch you, hear!
>
> Don't let sun's heat turn you dry.
> Don't let rain soak you.
> Don't let a thief rob you
> Or a stone bump your foot, hear!
> Walk well
> > Walk well
>
> *James Berry*

Comments

1 Your students may make errors constructing the negative form of these imperatives. Both of the following negative forms are correct:

Pattern 1: *Don't try to …*
Pattern 2: *Try not to …*

but modal verbs such as *must, can*, only use Pattern 3.

Pattern 3: *You can't/mustn't …*

Your students may use Pattern 1 incorrectly with modal verbs, for example:

Don't must be sad instead of *You mustn't be sad.*

2 This activity explores the language of giving advice, but the people we are advising are characters from folk and fairy tales, caught up in archetypal situations that reflect on our own lives, such as loveless marriages, enslavement, or journeys through lonely forests.

7.4 Celebrating and inviting poems: *Seeing snow*

Level Intermediate to advanced

Time 20 minutes

Aims To revise language for inviting and to learn vocabulary for organizing a party. Also to practise finding out about one another.

Materials

- For a lower-intermediate class, it may be helpful to bring to the class examples of real invitations, or to write an invitation to a party on a poster or on the blackboard.
- A more advanced class might enjoy the Sophie Hannah poem. It would be a good idea to have a written copy on a poster or projected on the wall while you read it out.

> **The End of Love**
>
> The end of love should be a big event.
> It should involve the hiring of a hall.
> Why the hell not? It happens to us all.
> Why should it pass without acknowledgement?
>
> Suits should be dry-cleaned, invitations sent.
> Whatever form it takes – a tiff, a brawl –
> The end of love should be a big event.
> It should involve the hiring of a hall.
>
> Better than the unquestioning descent
> Into the trap of silence, then the crawl
> From visible to hidden, door to wall.
>
> Get the announcements made, the money spent.
> The end of love should be a big event.
> It should involve the hiring of a hall.
>
> *Sophie Hannah*

Procedure

1 Ask your class to think of three events they would like to celebrate
which are usually forgotten or ignored. If your class are advanced
enough, you could read them the poem by Sophie Hannah and ask if
they could suggest other events such as 'the end of love' where it
would be nice to hire a hall. Here are some examples suggested by
classes:

the end of flu
my baby's first steps
understanding the news in English
the day my son made me a cup of tea
a card from a boy I like
seeing a rainbow
my first time seeing snow
my first grey hair

Explain they are going to organize a celebration for one of these
events: it could be a party, a meeting, a special meal, or anything else
they would like.

2 Choose one of the ideas they have suggested and build up with your
students a sample invitation, writing their suggestions on the
blackboard.

You are invited to celebrate …
Please wear …
Please bring …
Come to (a place) …
Come at (a time) …

When you have four or five completed sentences on the blackboard,
invite your students to choose one of the events they have listed and
write an invitation of their own. The poems can, of course, also be
written in pairs and groups. If there are causes for class celebration,
this is a good opportunity to bring it into the classroom and
acknowledge it. For example, *Eduardo has returned after a long absence;
everyone passed First Certificate.*

3 After ten minutes invite them to share and exchange their invitations
and choose one invitation they would like to accept. You could
include the following invitations, written by other students.

You are invited to
to celebrate seeing snow

Wear white
Wear warm clothes
Bring snowballs
Bring cameras
Bring sunglasses

Come to the mountain
At 6.00 to watch the first pieces fall.

You are invited to celebrate the end of flu

Bring blankets
paper to blow nose
a bottle of cough medicine
a good book to read

Sleeping will be 10 a.m.–11 p.m.
Medicine will be twice a day.
Come when you want!

Workshop poems

Variation

A more advanced class could write a short description, explaining why their event should be celebrated. Sophie Hannah's poem is an example of why we should celebrate the 'end of love'. Your students could write a 'free poem' explaining

- why they should celebrate seeing snow.
- why they should celebrate a baby's first steps, etc.

7.5 Poems comparing likes and preferences: *Tigers and oranges*

Level Elementary to advanced

Time 30 minutes

Aims To practise ways of expressing preference.

Preparation

1 Prepare a set of blank cards or pieces of paper for each student in your class.

2 You will need four or five large labels that can be folded to stand up on the desk. Write on each label one of the categories below. Choose categories in which your students have a good vocabulary.

Group 1: Animals
Group 2: Clothes
Group 3: Fruit
Group 4: Transport/Ways of travelling
Group 5: Things you see in cities
Group 6: Things you see in the countryside

Procedure

1 Divide your class into four groups and give each group one of the labels you have prepared. Large classes could have more groups, or more than one group sharing a category.

2 Give each group member a blank piece of paper. Ask them to write on their paper as many words as they can in their group category. They have two minutes to do so.

The following ideas may help them:

Animals	*fox, goat, tiger*
Clothes	*coat, trousers, skirt*
Fruit	*apple, mango, kiwi*
Food	*eggs, cheese, butter, sugar*
Ways of travelling (transport)	*bus, train, car*
Things you see in cities	*streets, cars, shops, houses, lamp posts*
Things you see in the countryside	*river, stream, hill, mountain, village*

3 After two minutes, stop the groups, and ask them to share their words with others in the group.

4 Now ask the class to look at the following structures. You could copy these on to the blackboard.

> I prefer _____ to _____
> I like _____ better than _____

They must finish the sentences, using the words their group have written. Ask the group to write at least four sentences using these words.

I prefer mangoes to oranges
I like tigers better than goats.

5 Now take in the words from each group and shuffle them, so the papers are in completely random order. Hand out a new card to each student. It is likely each group will now have a random set of words.

6 Invite group members to share their words with one another and to write a new set of preferences by mixing up all the categories. They will now produce 'wild' choices such as those in the second verse below:

> I prefer sandals to boots
> I prefer snow to mud
> I like music better than noise
> I like bicycles better than cars
> I like trees more than lamp-posts
> and peace better than war.
>
> I like oranges better than tigers
> I like mountains better than eggs
> I like honey better than traffic,
> I like rainbows better than cheese.
>
> *Workshop poem: Tokyo, Japan*

7 Ask the group to write poems with at least six sentences like the ones above. They can divide the sentences into verses:

- two verses of three lines each, or
- three verses of two lines each, or
- make up a pattern of their own, or
- make the last two lines in each verse rhyme.

A less advanced group may enjoy a middle stage after all the words have been shuffled and handed out to new students:

- Look at the words on your new list.
- If there are any words you don't know, check with others in your group and see if they can explain them.
- If there are any words you still don't know, miss them out and don't use them in your poem.

At the end of the lesson, you could go through these 'unknown' words, and ask the student who suggested it to offer an explanation.

Variations

A more advanced group may like to do this activity using abstract nouns instead of concrete nouns, to form exciting links between ideas: *I prefer shoes to poverty.*

Here are some examples:

> I prefer oranges to sadness
> I prefer laughter to tigers
> I like home better than houses

They may also like to listen to the song 'El Condor Pasa' by Paul Simon and Art Garfunkel and try out the pattern for themselves:

> I'd rather be a sparrow than a snail
> Yes I would, if I could
> I surely would

> I'd rather be a hammer than a nail
> Yes I would, if I could
> I surely would

Comments

Sometimes students may confuse the two structures:

I like … better than …
I prefer … to …

Typical errors are:

I like tigers to oranges
I prefer oranges better than sadness

Make sure the pattern is clear. Model this several times on the blackboard, and ask students to correct themselves if they still confuse the two structures.

7.6 Praise-songs: *My magnificent bull*

Level   Intermediate to advanced

Time   30 minutes

Aims   To practise and enrich vocabulary for complimenting, flattering, and praising.

Procedure

1   Choose one or more of the poems below to share with your students. Ask them to tell you:

What does the poet feel?
How do you know? What words does the poet use to show admiration?

Explain that this is the tradition of the African praise-song. Here you can make the beloved more wonderful and perfect than reality. To exaggerate, flatter, praise, and compliment is all part of the praise-song culture.

> **My Magnificent Bull**
>
> My bull is white like the silver fish in the river,
> White like the shimmering crane bird on the river bank
> White like fresh milk!
> His roar is like thunder to the Turkish cannon on the steep
>   shore.
> My bull is dark like the raincloud in the storm.
> He is like summer and winter.
> Half of him is dark like the storm cloud
> Half of him is light like the sunshine.
> His back shines like the morning star.
> His brow is red like the back of the hornbill.
> His forehead is like a flag, calling the people from a
>   distance.
> He resembles the rainbow.
> I will water him at the river,
> With my spear I shall drive my enemies.
> Let them water their herds at the well;
> The river belongs to me and my bull.
> Drink, my bull, from the river; I am here
> to guard you with my spear.
>
> *Traditional from the Dinka*

Inspectors coming to visit our teacher

How kind you are, oh inspector!
You are as wise as an old tree!
You are as brave as a warrior!
What a large red pen you have!
What are you writing?
Your words are so golden!

To the First Certificate examiner

Oh sweet examiner
How clever you are!
How just you are!
You are as good as a grandmother!
You are as kind as a nurse!
Now please help me pass my exam!

Teaching practice class, Madrid, Spain

2 Now ask your students to think about what they would like to praise in this way and share their ideas with a neighbour.

These are some ideas suggested by classes:

my cat
a horse
my wife
my wedding dress
my grandmother
my running shoes

3 Collect on the blackboard words used to praise something adored. Ask the students what words they would use to do this.

Write as many words as the class can suggest in five minutes. The following suggestions may be useful.

| You are
Your words are
Your thoughts are
Your deeds are
Your eyes are
Your smile is
Your voice is
Your breath is
Your open hand is | (as) | wonderful
sweet
glorious
clever
beautiful
magnificent
superb
brave
just
strong
noble | (as a _____) |

4 Read the list aloud with your students chanting or beating the words like a song.

5 Now ask your students to work in a group of four or five. They are going to write a praise-song for their beloved person/object/animal using the words and structures above as a starting point.

They can also use phrases to address their beloved:

Oh wonderful one!
Oh perfect one!
You who are so great!

6 Give the class 15 minutes to write their praise-songs. They can write the lines in groups of four using a different adjective in each line:

My running shoes are as magnificent as two white birds
as bright as two stars
as fast as an athlete

or using the same adjective in each line:

My cat is as beautiful as a queen
as beautiful as a princess
as beautiful as my friend

or introducing an address between each verse:

Oh magnificent cat!

7 For classes where a little noise is permitted, and students who enjoy 'theatre', invite the groups to perform their songs:

- using their different voices for each line
- joining in all together for some lines
- cheering, dancing, and singing when the name of the beloved is mentioned.

If time is a little short you can begin the next lesson with this.

Follow-up

1 A follow-up or development of this activity, would involve looking at the parts of the beloved:

> *her whiskers are white like snow*
> *her paws are soft like velvet*
> *her eyes are green like the sea*

2 Advanced classes may enjoy some modern examples of the praise-song:

> And I think to myself
> What a wonderful world!
> *Louis Armstrong*

Comments

Praise-song is the practice of wild and joyful compliments for leaders, beloved objects, and beloved people. Traditionally the praise-song would have been danced with beating drums and gorgeous costumes to accompany the words.

8
Genre poems

All language has the quality of a poem: the way it is set out on the page, the length of lines, the choice of words and structures all help us to understand its purpose. Lists, memos, application forms, diaries, letters, recipes, and postcards all have their special features. We can recognize them almost at a glance, and understand who wrote the message and why. A list will probably be in a long thin line, with words on their own rather than in structures or in sentences. A picture postcard is likely to be informal and friendly, with special formulae for opening or closing. Some of these texts even suggest to us the work we must do as a reader: we must complete application forms (usually), we must reply to memos, we must buy the products on the list. Just as in a good poem, the writer engages the reader in a lively interaction: read me, and I will make something change!

This chapter looks at these familiar signs of a 'text' or 'genre': written language that gives clear messages about *who, where*, and *why* it has been written. We play with the language and layout particular to each, but stretch them just a little further, so they become fantasy, wordplay, language game, or exploration.

Some of the examples given in these activities are 'real' lists, diaries, or memos. That is, they have been plucked out of everyday life, and placed on the page, just as a pebble from the beach may be placed in a museum case, or a leaf from a tree may be placed in a picture frame. What happens to these objects in their strange new places is that we look at them freshly and carefully. We notice how interesting the words of the list might be; how rich or surprising the ideas are sitting next to one another on the paper. This kind of poem is called a **found poem**, because it has been 'found' and borrowed from the everyday world. It is something your students will be able to do too, as they become more confident with the language.

8.1 Recipe poems: *Custard kisses*

Level   Intermediate to advanced

Time   20 minutes

Aims   To practise the language of instructions. To learn the vocabulary of cooking

Preparation

Copy the chart below to share with your students. Choose the words in each column which your students will understand, and add others of your own.

Verbs	Cooking ingredients
mix	onions
cut	custard
chop	lemon juice
grind	sugar
fold in	flour
sprinkle	butter
squeeze	grated cheese
slice	eggs

Procedure

1 Ask the students to look at the words on the board. *What are they all about? Have you ever used a recipe to cook? To bake? Have you ever written a recipe?*

Invite your class to remember these words, and add more words to each of the lists.

2 Now explain they are not going to make a cake, but one of the items below.
- *a good friendship or marriage*
- *a love potion/drink for a boyfriend or girlfriend*
- *an intelligence potion/drink to pass exams*
- *a beauty potion/drink*

Ask the class to vote on which item they would like to make. Choose one as a class poem.

3 To make this drink, what ingredients are needed? This time the ingredients will be qualities, experiences. Here are some suggestions made by other students who have tried out this activity.

'Life' ingredients
kindness
jokes
kisses
tears
forgiveness

Invite your students to add more ideas of their own.

4 Use the students' ideas to build a class poem. Each line should include a verb and an ingredient: either a 'food' ingredient or a 'life' ingredient, or a combination of the two.

Stir in custard kisses
Sprinkle sugar jokes
Mix with onion tears

5 Divide the class into groups of two or three. Ask each group to choose their own item to make. They can choose another one from the list in Point 2 above, or something of their own.

6 Ask each group to write their own poem, using the same pattern as the class poem.

7 When the groups have finished, they can read their poems aloud or share them with another group. An interesting extension task is for the rest of the class to guess the title for the poem.

Here are examples of poems written by Malaysian students in Plymouth which you could share.

Eternal Stirfry

Heat 2 tablespoons of sizzling kisses
in a non-stick marriage vow.
Gently mix finely chopped white commitment
with diced honesty.
Stir until the aroma blossoms.
Pour sauce. Add green jealousy.
Sprinkle childish innocence and sliced laughter.
Avoid black faithlessness: it might ruin the taste.

Valentine-stockings custard

4 cups of happy thoughts
1 cup of faith flour
1 cup of condensed tears
1 cup of jealousy
and fruits of love.

Mix all the ingredients in a wishing pot.
Stir with Cupid's ladle.
Pour the mixture into a pair of love stockings.
Freeze in the heavenly pole.

Malaysian students in Plymouth, UK

Variation

You could adapt this activity if you think cookery won't be popular with all the class, by changing the verbs and ingredients to be about making and building a machine, for example. Many of the verbs in the box above will still be useful, and you can add others, such as: *attach, connect.*

Comments

Focus here on the accurate use of simple instructions. The verbs do not need to be changed at all.

Mix, cut, chop, grind

Other structures your students could use:

You must …
You should …

A very informal way of giving instructions is in the simple present:

You cut …
You chop …
You grind … , etc.

All of these are correct. However, it is best to use only one of these forms in the recipe. If your students use more than one, ask them to choose which they prefer, and to use that form consistently all the way through.

8.2 Memo poems: *I have forgotten to take the rose*

Level Lower-intermediate to advanced

Time 20 minutes

Aims To practise the language of simple messages and notes.

Preparation

Below are some typical phrases used in short messages. Choose several of these and write them on the blackboard at the start of the activity.

Just a note to tell you …
A quick message to let you know …
Sorry, I forgot to …
Gone home.
Supper in fridge.
Feed cat.
Ring your mum.
Arrived safely.
Thanks for the meal.
See you tomorrow at 5.00.

Procedure

1 Ask your students to look at the phrases on the blackboard. *Where would you see or hear them?* Here are some possibilities:

on the fridge door
a text message on the mobile phone
a recorded telephone message
a note pushed under the door

Write their ideas on the blackboard.

2 Discuss with your students the following: *when did you last write messages like these, and who to?* Ask the students to share their ideas with a partner.

3 Invite the group to share some of their answers to the questions. Write on the board some of the 'short message' situations which they describe:

- letting friends know you have arrived home after a journey
- leaving a message for a housemate to say someone phoned for them
- confirming an arrangement with a friend
- leaving a message for a housemate about household jobs that must be done
- telling someone you have safely received their gift or message
- thanking someone for a gift, or a meal, or a nice evening
- telling someone you have left something behind in their home
- telling someone you have forgotten to do a job you had promised to do

4 Ask the students to choose one of the situations from the list, and write a short memo or message.

5 After ten minutes, invite them to share their messages with a neighbour. See if the neighbour can guess the situation. *Who is the message written for, and why?*

Variation

An interesting variation, to show how 'reduced' a message can be, is to elicit complete sentences, such as:

I've caught the 6.00 train and will phone you when I arrive.

Write the sentence on the board.

Then discuss with your students which words can be cut out, so the message is still clear. Rub out each word as it is suggested. A 'minimum' version of this one could be:

Caught 6.00 train. I'll phone.

Follow-up

Collect all the poems, shuffle them up, and give each student someone else's poem.
Their task is to read the memo, and write a short note in reply.

Your students may also enjoy reading the following poems, and comparing them to their own.

> I have forgotten to take the rose
> the rose
> which is on my desk
> and which
> you probably saw in the morning
>
> *Miranda, Greek student, Plymouth, UK*

I failed to put this
in a cover and mail –
sorry, sorry, sorry

Indian student, Chidambaram, India

The Figs and Biscuits

I've just eaten the figs and biscuits I was keeping
    for you when you came
When I realized you weren't coming
I figured I might as well.

They were all good, but frankly,
there was twice as much as I wanted.

I think I'm going to be lovesick.

David Bateman from Eating your Cake and Having It

Comments

Although memos can be very short, with just key words, the message as a whole needs to make sense. The best way to check this is to ask students to read their messages to one another.

Can the partner guess the context for the message?

If the answer is YES, then the message has worked.

If the answer is NO, then invite the partners to change the message so there is enough information in it to be meaningful.

8.3 List poems: *Tom's Blue-eye astrologer's shop*

Level Elementary to advanced

Time 20 minutes

Aims To practise vocabulary in lexical sets. To practise classifying and grouping words.

Preparation

Check **found poems** in the glossary.

Procedure

1 Invite your students to read/listen to one or two of the classroom poems below.

What do they notice about the poems? Encourage them to notice the following features of lists:

• there are no complete sentences
• there are articles in the lists, but no verbs.

India

a painting on silk
a necklace of marigolds
a handful of spices
tea leaves
a stick of incense
a coloured bangle
chapattis
a palace
a temple
a lake
the banyan tree
Tom's Blue-Eye astrologer's shop

Kossuth Street, Pecs, Hungary

Hungarian ice-cream shop
Consom supermarket
Kwikfit shoe shop
a delicatessen with cheese and cream
the opera house in cream
the Palatina hotel with tables in the courtyard
the cinema down a lane
the sports shop
the electrical shop
the cake and coffee shop as old as the Turks

Workshop poems from Hungary and India

2 Ask students to think of where they come from. If they were writing
a list that showed the smells, colours, objects, and history of their
own town, what would they include? Or if they were to fill a box with
items that reminded them of home, what would they include? Elicit
their ideas and write these on the board.

3 Now write on the board the possible lists below, and add others of
your own. Invite your class to work in groups of two and three. Each
group should choose a list and write down as many items as they can
in ten minutes.

> - Time capsule: put in a box 20 items that would tell people in 1000 years' time what your life is like now.
> - Desert island box: what would you take with you to a desert island.
> - Treasure trove: if you found a box of treasure, what would you most like to be inside it?
> - Picnic box: if you put together the perfect picnic basket, what would be inside it?
> - Travel kit: if you went away for one month, what would you take in your travel kit?
> - List of shops in the high street.
> - List of jobs of each person in your street.

4 After ten minutes, invite groups to read their lists to one another and suggest a title for each list.

Variation

An interesting variation of this activity is to ask your students to find a list in English: ingredients on the back of a food product, list of items in an insurance policy, list of TV programmes in the newspaper, list of books on a bookshelf and write these down as a found poem. They can reorganize the lines to make them more interesting.

Below is an example of a found list: these are all poems about love, 'found' in the index of a poetry book.

> **Love**
>
> Love bade me welcome; yet my soul drew back
> Love guards the roses of thy lips
> Love in fantastic triumph sate.
> Love in my bosom like a bee
> Love is a sickness full of woes
> Love is and was my Lord and King
> Love is enough; though the World be a-waning
> Love is the blossom where there blows
> Love not me for comely grace
> Love, thou art absolute, sole Lord
> Love wing'd my Hopes and taught me how to fly
> Lully, lulley; lully, lulley
>
> *John Daniel, found in index to Oxford Book of English Verse*

Comments

The main language your students will need are nouns. Help them to find the right noun, by using a dictionary if necessary.

8.4 Diary poems: *First pair of high heels*

Level Elementary to intermediate

Time 20 minutes

Aims To practise the simple past. To practise different ways of writing the date.

Procedure

1 Ask the class to tell you the date of their birthdays. Write some of these dates on the blackboard.

2 Now ask your students to think about their last birthday.
What is one thing you remember about your last birthday?
It could be a present you received, something you did, what someone did or said, a card or a note you received.

3 After two minutes, ask your students to share their memories, and write some of these on the blackboard.

4 Now ask your class to remember four birthdays. They could be
birthdays I remember: some good, some bad! OR
birthdays that were special in some way

Ask your students to choose.

5 For each birthday, ask them to write just one diary entry with a memory of that day. The diary entry should start with a note of the date and year. As before, it could be:

a memory of a gift or present
a memory of a person: what they said, did or wrote
a memory of what you did on that day

The memory can be written in short note form with just key words:

August 17th 2000: 6.00 p.m. Party

or it can be written in short sentences, using the present tense for vivid storytelling:

November 9th 1999: I have my first driving lesson

or it can be written in note form, using verbs without pronouns:

February 18th: Went swimming after school

or it can be a full and detailed description, using the simple past and complete sentences.

Choose the note form that suits the level of your class.

Below are examples of presents for each birthday:

April 17th 1965 a chocolate rabbit
April 17th 1970 paints and a paintbrush
April 17th 1975 first pair of high heels
April 17th 1980 my school graduation
April 17th 1985 an engagement ring
April 17th 1990 my first baby

June 20th 1981   birthday cake shaped like a train
June 20th 1984   white trainers
June 20th 1989   first kiss
June 20th 1992   first driving lesson
June 20th 1997   first job interview
June 20th 1999   no presents, but a job, a car, and a
                  girlfriend

6   After ten minutes, invite each student to read their diary entries to a
    partner. Invite some students to read their lines to others in the class.

Variation

Other variations of this activity could be:

*   Choose a favourite month of the year. Write one sentence for
    different memories of this month in four different years.
*   A festival in four different years.
*   An anniversary in four different years.

Comments

The main areas for accuracy in this activity are:

1   The way the month is written. Here are the different methods:

*   using numbers only:
    in British English the numbers are day/month/year (9/11/65)
    in American English the numbers are month/day/year (11/9/65)
*   using words and numbers: 9 November 1965 OR November 9 1965
*   using ordinal numbers and words: 9th November 1954

2   The main tense that should follow the date is the simple past.

8.5   Postcard poems: *Greetings from the moon*

Level   Lower-intermediate to intermediate

Time   20 minutes

Aims   To practise sending short messages. To practise formulae for
informal greetings.

Materials

*   The picture on the next page.
*   Postcards you have received from friends on holiday.

Procedure

1   Ask your students to look at the picture on the next page. *What do you
    think the man on the deckchair might be writing?* Invite them to suggest
    some words or phrases and write these on the board.

2 Show the class some postcards that you have received. Pass them round the class, and ask your students to notice if there any other interesting or useful phrases they could use on a postcard.

Below is a chart you might build up with your students on the board.

Dear _____	
Greetings from ...	
I wish you could	see
	hear
It's been great to	feel
It's been such fun to	eat
	drink
Tomorrow I will	meet
	visit
I'd better finish now.	
I'm going to	

3 You could also use the sample 'postcard poems' below as examples, but take care – they were written by elementary language learners and there are some errors. You may want to correct these, or invite your students to do so.

Do they use any of the predicted phrases? What do they do that is typical of postcards?

- start with a greeting
- list things you have done and seen, and people you have met
- use the simple past to describe these things
- end with future plans.

Dear my father
Greetings from my classroom.
I wish you could tell me the answers.
It's been great to meet English person.
It's been great to make poems,
It's been great to learn football.
It's been great to eat fish and chip.
I am not good student.
Tomorrow I will be good.

Bedford primary language centres

Greetings from the moon,
I wish you could see all the moon people.
They look like you!
We visited the space station.
We met the Chief.
We saw earth through a big machine.
We saw big smoke over city.
Tomorrow I will fly home.

Haringey primary school

4   Now explain that your students are going to write their own fantasy postcards.

Invite them to complete the phrase *Greetings from …* with a fantasy phrase of their own choice. The phrase can be followed by either a person or a place.

Greetings from the moon.
Greetings from the centre of the earth.
Greetings from Manchester United.
Greetings from a character in a film, story, or folk tale: write the postcard as that character.
Greetings from a favourite or famous world landmark.

Write their suggestions on the board.

Below are some that were suggested by classes:

Greetings from Hogwarts School (Harry Potter's school).
Greetings from a bunker (an underground hiding place) *in the mountains.*
Greetings from the Titanic.
Greetings from Tutankhamen.

5   Now invite the class to work in groups of two and three to finish the 'postcard'. The phrases you have built up on the board can help them.

6   When they have finished, invite students to 'post' their cards to other students in the class, or display them around the room and write replies to one another.

Follow-up

Ask your students to make and write real postcards to send to their friends and family.

8.6 Answerphone messages: *Press nothing*

Level Lower-intermediate to advanced

Time 20 minutes

Aims To practise the language used in formal recorded answerphone messages.

Preparation

1 If you can, tape yourself or a colleague reading a typical recorded message, and play this to your students at the beginning of the lesson. You could write your own answerphone script, or tape one of the classroom poems below, using a formal 'answerphone' voice.

> If you would like information about your future, press 1.
> If you would like it to be good news, press 2.
> If you would like it to be bad news, press 3.
> If you would like it to be about your study, press 4.
> If you would like it to be about your love, press 5.
> If you would like it to be about money, press 6.
> If none of these, please wait to be connected.
>
> If you would like to be surprised, press 1.
> If you would like to be excited, press 2.
> If you would like to be frightened, press 3.
> If you would like to be amused, press 4.
> If you would like to be, press 5.
> If you would like not to be, press nothing.
>
> *Workshop poems*

2 Prepare on the blackboard one or two phrases which will 'set the scene' for the recorded message or answerphone. Choose those you think will be most helpful for your students.

This is a recorded message.
I'm afraid we cannot answer your call at the moment.
We are unable to take your call at the moment.
If you would like _____, press _____
If none of these, please wait to be connected.

Procedure

1 Show your students the key sentences on the blackboard, or play them your answerphone tape. Ask them to tell you where they might hear these phrases. Ask your class to be specific about where they hear answerphone messages. Typical answers might be:

phoning for train or bus timetables
phoning a cinema for cinema times
phoning a bank
phoning a travel agency
phoning for a weather forecast

but this, of course, will depend on what is most common in your students' own lives. Write their suggestions on the blackboard.

2   Choose one of the contexts from the list above, or one elicited by your students. Ask them to suggest as many possible ways as they can for completing the sentence below:

If you would like … press (a number).

Write their ideas on the blackboard.

Phoning for a train timetable

If you would like to travel to Delhi, press 1.
If you would like to travel to Madras, press 2.
If you would like to travel to Ooty, press 3.

When you have four or five examples on the blackboard, read the sentences aloud with your class.

3   Now divide the class into groups of two or three. Give each group one of the contexts, and ask them to write as many answerphone lines as they can for their context. Give the groups ten minutes to do this.

If you have a large class, ask them to work in larger groups of four or five.

With a less advanced class, each group could write answerphone lines for the same context.

4   After ten minutes, ask each group to join up with two others, and to mix up their answerphone lines so the context becomes jumbled. For example:

If you would like to know about weather in Paris, press 1.
If you would like a train to Amritsar, press 2.
If you would like to know about Thursday films, press 3.

5   Ask the groups to experiment with strange and interesting ways of combining their lines. When they are ready, invite them to read their answerphone messages to the rest of the class.

Comments

This activity is relevant for students who listen to recorded telephone messages and may need to hear them in English.

If this is not a typical situation for your students, the memo activity (8.2) may be more suitable. This is designed to practise short written notes and messages.

8.7 Greetings card jumble poem: *Merry birthday*

Level Elementary to intermediate

Time 20 minutes

Aims To notice short conventional phrases used in greetings cards, and short messages. To notice typical collocations, and what happens to meaning when these are changed.

Preparation

1 Ask students to bring to the class examples of birthday, festival, and greetings cards.

2 Check **collocations** in the glossary.

Procedure

1 If the students have brought cards, display these around the room or ask students to pass them around, so everyone can read them.

2 Ask students to share as many phrases as they know for writing in greetings cards. Where possible, translate mother tongue phrases into English, or choose an equivalent from the list below. Write these phrases up on the board.

Happy birthday
Many thanks
Merry Christmas
Season's greetings
Holiday greetings
Many apologies
Good luck
Congratulations
Well done
Enjoy your holiday
Happy anniversary/Eid/Chanukah/Diwali/New Year

---

3 Now explain you are going to experiment with the phrases, by jumbling them all up and seeing what happens. The rules are:

- make new combinations by moving words around
- jumble up the different greetings to make new ones
- make sure the combinations all work grammatically.

Here is an example:

Birthday poem

Merry birthday!
Enjoy your birthday!
Good birthday
Lucky birthday

4 Elicit some other changes and combinations, and write these on the board.

Even though the combinations are unusual, they should still be grammatically correct. Invite your students to notice which combinations are, or are not, grammatically correct:

Many luck : 'many' is for countable nouns, 'luck' is uncountable.
Happy your holiday: pronouns must come first in the phrase.
Well thanks: 'well' is an adverb, not an adjective.

5 Now divide the class into groups of two or three. Each group should prepare a short poem which uses four or five different combinations of words.

Variations

A variation for more advanced learners would be to select a recipient for the greetings card and make the message more personal:

- an apology to one's pet after a long holiday away
- a greeting to a pot plant after a day at work
- a goodbye to clothes being given to a charity shop
- a thank you to a pickpocket for reminding you to be more careful.

9

Poetry games

The activities in this chapter are divided into two types. Activities 9.1, 9.2, and 9.3 are group poems, which are built up round the class by each person contributing a line or an idea. It depends on the mix of different people and thoughts, and the outcome is always unpredictable. These activities are excellent for building up a sense of team spirit, for breaking the ice, or for bringing a lesson to a close. The outcomes, unlike usual warm-ups, can be kept, reread, read aloud, and discussed in future lessons for language and content.

The second set of activities, 9.4 and 9.5, experiment with letters, words, and poems as pictures that can be set out on the page in unusual formations. The way they look on the page can be part of their message. These are called **concrete poems**, because they shape words visually just like an object we can touch and hold. For example, Wes McGee wrote a poem in the shape of Africa; Lewis Carroll wrote a poem in the shape of a cat's long tail. Combining words with shapes and visual images is an interesting way to learn new vocabulary and to fix ideas in the memory. It is also something that students with very little English are able to do.

The final activity, 9.6, is a guessing game. The poem is a secret which the reader has to guess. This kind of poem is also part of a much-loved tradition, the **riddle**, in which the writer plays a game with the reader … *guess who I am.*

9.1 Mini-sagas: *There was a boy from Turkey*

Level Lower-intermediate to advanced

Time 25 minutes

Aims To practise the language of narrative. To describe the story process (opening, development, ending).

Procedure

1 Write the phrases below on the blackboard and ask your students where they would see these. They might answer: *a story, a joke*.

> 1 Once upon a time
> 2 Then
> 3 He said
> 4 She said
> 5 Finally/Now

2 Explain that the class is going to tell a story in just five sentences. Each sentence will start with one of the phrases on the board.

Elicit one or more 'mini-sagas' from the class, by asking them to complete each sentence round the class.

3 Now divide the class into groups of five, and ask each group member to finish Sentence 1 at the top of a blank sheet of paper.

Once upon a time …

4 They should then pass the paper to their neighbour, who writes Sentence 2.

Then …

5 Pass the paper round until all five sentences have been written and each group member has their own paper back again.

Advanced learners may want to spend a long time writing after each phrase. This can make the activity lose pace. Here are several strategies you could use:

- limit each stage of writing to one minute. Explain this at the beginning, and stop each stage after one minute is over.
- limit each stage of writing to just one new idea expressed as a phrase, a few key words, or a sentence.

6 Give students the opportunity to read out their mini-sagas to the rest of the class.

Variations

1 In the 'Consequences' game variation of this activity, each group member folds over the paper so their sentence is secret. This can result in funny and bizarre sets of sentences which students often enjoy.

2 You could use other key phrases to introduce the stages of the story. For example:

Once upon a time there was …
One day …
The next day …
After that …
In the end …

3 A variation for adult learners who may want a more 'down to earth' approach is to make this poem simply the record of an interesting conversation.

One day I met …
He/she said …
I said …
He/she said …
I said …
Then …

Here is an example, written by a poet who is also a busy librarian.

> Half-way to work this morning I met John.
> We walked a yard or two together. I
> was late and hurrying, and John said, 'Why
> this most unseemly haste? What's going on?'
> I looked at him and thought. The sun shone.
> He was just as late and in no hurry.
> I saw the point. I said, 'Why should we worry?
> How old's the human race, one million,
> two million years? And after all that time
> we're scared of being a minute late!' I slowed.
> Bit of perspective, eh?' said John. 'Indeed!
> What's lateness after all?' I said. 'A crime?'
> Then John turned left down Pennsylvania Road.
> I sauntered on a while – then picked up speed.
>
> *James Turner, Exeter*

Comments

1 Stories usually use the simple past tense. The phrase *Once upon a time* suggests the use of the past tense.

However, your students may notice that many jokes and stories told orally use the simple present:

He says … Then she says …

This is a correct and acceptable use of the present simple. Allow your students to use this if they wish to, but take care that the time phrases they use do not suggest the past, as in *Once upon a time*.

2 A mini-saga tells a story in a nutshell. In just a few sentences, a mini-saga can trace the development of a character or a situation, and make us see 'a world in a grain of sand'. A perfect mini-saga has 50 words in it, like the example on the next page by Eugene Larger.

Once upon a time
A man fell in love
He courted
Finally winning her
Married
They grew accustomed to each other
He noticed the change
Her countenance fallen
He asked what was wrong
She said, 'I don't know.'
He asked, 'Do you love me?'
She said, 'Once upon a time.'

Eugene Lager, Mexico

Once upon a time
there was a boy from Turkey.
Then he came to Germany.
Then he came to England.
Then he was very confused.
He said, 'I am confused!'
The teacher said, 'It will be OK!'
Now he waits for it to be OK.

Turkish learner, Bedford language centre

9.2 Chain poems: *Snake in the grass*

Level   Lower-intermediate to advanced

Time   20 minutes

Aims   To practise building sentences. To look at the links in meaning between words.

Preparation
Take a copy of the Workshop poems listed in the procedure point 1 below to share with your class, either on a poster or on the board.

Procedure
1   Show the class the following poems. Ask if they notice anything unusual about the poems.

Letters make words.
Words make phrases.
Phrases make paragraphs.
Paragraphs make compositions.
Compositions make books.
Books tell us
very important things.

Eduardo Gonzalez Chillon, Spain

Money is such a problem
Problem is we never find it
It is such a snake
Snake runs into the grass
Grass disappears
Disappears like our money

Air became breath
Breath became words
Words became a song
Song became air

Workshop poems

2   Explain that you are going to build a poem round the class. Choose one of the words suggested below, which have worked well to start poems.

Money, Sun, Classrooms, Holidays, Parents, Learning, English, Air, Water, Earth, Mud, Stone, Song

Give the first line yourself as a starting point or ask the class to think about one, and choose one of your students to start.

3   Build the poem around the class, and keep a note of the poem as it grows.

Don't worry if students change the form of the link words, for example a verb changes tense, or a noun moves from singular to plural. Keep a written note as the poem develops, and use these changes as teaching points for discussion.

4   Let the poem come to a natural end. As soon as it becomes difficult, after five, seven, or ten lines, finish the 'poem' and start another one with the same starting word.

5   Now invite your students to work in groups of four, five, and six. Each group should choose a starting word from the list above, and go round the group, building one line each and using the same rules. Each four, five, or six lines is one verse.

6   For an enthusiastic class, invite them to add a final line, which ends with the word they started with, like the two classroom examples.

Comments

Depending on the level of the class, you could:

- ask group members to check that all the suggested lines are grammatically correct
- allow errors, as long as the lines make sense
- allow just phrases and key words
- ask for complete sentences only.

This poetry game is designed to be 'written' by a group, with each member suggesting the next line of the poem, based on the word that went before.

This encourages students to listen hard to one another, and to help one another where the structures become difficult. The emphasis is on making words and ideas link with one another. The teacher needs to stand back, and notice the kind of structures and vocabulary which learners choose and the kind of errors that emerge. These too are unpredictable, and will be directed by the knowledge and skills of your students.

9.3 Expanding poems: *Roses at the wedding*

Level   Lower-intermediate to advanced

Time   20 minutes

Aims   To practise building sentences (complex and co-ordinate sentences).

Preparation

Check **co-ordinate clause** and **subordinate clause** in the glossary.

Procedure

1   Write on the blackboard one of the topics below.

> People at a party
> *I went to the party and I saw …*
>
> Walking down a street: shops, people, events:
> *I went down the road and I saw …*
>
> Shopping for presents
> *I went to the shops and I bought …*
> *For my birthday I asked for …*

2   Explain you are going to build a 'growing' class poem together. Ask your students to look at the topic on the blackboard, and suggest the first sentence.
Write the first sentence on the board. For example:

I went to the party and I saw a girl with purple hair.

Now start the poem-building around the class. Choose the next student, and ask him/her to repeat the line on the blackboard, and then add a new one. Write this new line on the board.

I went to the party and I saw a girl with purple hair and purple fingernails.

The new line need not be a new sentence. Instead your students can make the sentence that is already there 'grow'. *How can you make a sentence grow?*

- by adding 'and' with a new clause or a new phrase
- by adding 'but' with a new clause
- by adding a relative pronoun which is the start of a new clause:
  who, what, where, when

- by adding a wide range of conjunctions, which introduce a subordinate clause: *because, so, as, since, while, although.*

If your students run out of ideas, invite them

- to start a new sentence
- to use one of the conjunctions or relative pronouns. These words are very useful in setting up a new 'train of thought'.

3 Choose the next learner, and ask him/her to repeat the two lines on the board and add a third one.

I went to the party and I saw a girl with purple hair
and purple fingernails
and a ring through her nose.

4 Once your students have got the idea, move around the class, with each student adding a new line. If the topic dries up, stop it and start a new one.

5 Now divide the class into groups of four or five. Write the other topics on the board, and ask each group to choose one.

6 When they are ready ask them to 'write' an expanding poem in the same way as they have just done with the whole class.

i.e. one person says the first line
their neighbour repeats the first line and says a second one
and so on around the group.

Variation

This activity is initially an oral one, and can be played without any writing. However, a variation could be a written version, each group writing their poem with 'growing' verses, as in the wedding poem below. You could copy this and display it on the wall as an example.

The wedding

Roses at the wedding.

Roses at the wedding
and lanterns in the trees.

Roses at the wedding
and lanterns in the trees
and children played in the fountains

Roses at the wedding
and lanterns in the trees
and children played in the fountains
and the flute began to play

Roses at the wedding
and lanterns in the trees
and children played in the fountains
and the flute began to play
as the bride sailed in.

9.4 Shape poems: *Write my country*

Level Elementary to advanced

Time 30 minutes

Aims To look at language for describing places and landscapes. To experiment with the shape and layout of words.

Materials

- If you can, prepare a set of blank labels for your students, with tape or some other way of attaching them to your country outline.
- An atlas of the world with large maps of the countries where your students come from would also be helpful in this activity. If all your students are from the same country, draw a large map (outline only) of their country for them to copy.
- Large pieces of paper will be useful in the group activity – the larger the paper, the better.

Preparation

1 Bring to the class, or draw on the blackboard, a large outline of the country where you are teaching.

2 The language suggested by classes in this activity has been exciting and surprising. However, if you would like to guide their vocabulary, below are some suggestions which you could prepare on the board or on a wall display.

COLOURS
green   yellow   orange   blue   turquoise   white   grey
black   navy   purple

OPPOSITES
quiet: crowded/loud/busy
safe: dangerous
large: small

PLACES
forest   mountain   river   valley   desert   city   village
coast   sea   beach   cliffs   lake

Procedure

1 Ask your students to look on the blackboard at your outline and tell you what they see.

our country
a map
an outline of where we are

2 Ask your students to suggest words you could put into the outline to explain what is inside the country. You are not asking for the names of towns and cities, but the names of types of landscape, feelings, colours, fruits, customs.

The words should be *adjective* + *noun*.

For example:

the dry horizon
the drugged sands
the screaming thunder
the hazy river
the heavenly food

3   Ask your students if they can suggest where on the map the words should go. Is there a special place on the map for 'purple mountain', for example?

4   Distribute the blank labels to your students, so each has at least one. Ask them to write another phrase about the country, and to stick it on the map where they think it should belong.

5   If your students are from many different countries, ask them to work with people from the same country, or to join a group who share knowledge of one country. Ask them to draw an outline of their country – a very loose one is adequate.

If your class has groups unevenly representing different homelands, here are some suggestions:

- divide the class into even groups and ask each to draw a map of the country where they are studying OR
- ask the class to work in groups of two or three with students who are not from the same country. Each student should draw a loose outline of their own country. When they have finished, they should exchange outlines with their partner, on their partner's map and mark with an X the places which they would like described. Back with their own country outline, each group member should write an *adjective* + *noun* description beside all the Xs marked on their maps.

6   Invite them to write their phrases on the map.

7   When they are ready, display the maps on the walls and ask the groups to circulate and read one another's maps. This is an excellent awareness-raising activity for students to learn about one another and their countries of birth.

Variations

You can use the 'shape' idea for many other kinds of poems. An outline of their country has been a particularly successful shape with adult learners, especially when they are learning English away from their homeland and are in multicultural groups. However, other variations which work well are:

a map of the inside of my head
a map of my bedroom

9.5 Alphabet poems: *H is the high jump*

Level Elementary to intermediate

Time 25 minutes

Aims To invite students to look more closely at the alphabet. To develop mnemonics for writing the letters.

Procedure

1 Show your students the picture at the beginning of this activity or draw a few letters of the alphabet on the board. These could be both the letters of the Roman alphabet and those of the mother tongue alphabet if this is different.

2 Ask your students to look at the letters.

What does each letter look like in the picture?
Could those letters be drawn in any other way?
What about the other letters in the alphabet? What do they look like?

Give them some examples. Below are suggestions by students:

> A is a tent
> B is a fat lady
> C is the moon
> D is a man with a big stomach
> E are 3 bookshelves
> F is a gallows
> H is the high jump
>
> *Workshop poem*

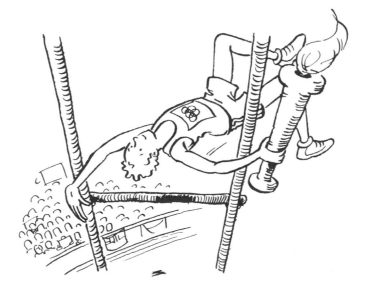

Every letter
means or appears to mean something.
A is the first, the director.
B is the servant of the leader.
C is a lodestone.
D is a semicircle.
E is a fork without a handle.
F is a television aerial.
G is a dangerous curve.
H is a rugby goalpost
I is a straight line.
J is a hook.
K is one line with victory on its side.
L is a corner.
M is like two mountains.
N is Zorro asleep.
O is a circle.
P is a flag.
Q is a circle with one foot.
R is a 'P'; with a lame leg
S is the sign of Superman.
T is a telegraph pole.
U is a lodestone on its side.
V is the sign of peace.
W is a double victory.
X marks the place.
Y is an aerial on Mars.
Z is the sign of Zorro.

Eduardo Gonzalez Chillon, Spain

3 Elicit ideas for the first five or six letters of the alphabet and write these on the blackboard.

4 Now divide the class into pairs. Ask each partner to write their names, with one letter on each line like this:

R
E
Z
A

and pass their paper to their neighbour.

5 The neighbour must complete each letter in the same way.

R is a large lady doing a dance
E is a thin man sitting down and holding out his arms
Z is the path to my house
A is a tent

Variations

There is an interesting variation of this activity for students who do not share the same alphabet. Invite them to draw the letters of their alphabet and describe what each of these looks like.

In some cases there may be a mnemonic which helped them to learn the letter when they were first learning to write.

In the case of Chinese characters there will be 'real' pictures which letters represent.

For students still mastering the formation of letters, the task could be to contrast upper- and lower-case letters. Upper-case letters are capital letters, LIKE THIS.
Lower-case letters are small letters, like this.

e is a round man sitting down
E is a thin man sitting down

Comments

For students mastering the alphabet, the formation of the letters is the area to correct for accuracy.

However, this activity can also encourage vocabulary enrichment for more advanced learners. At this level, encourage students to work together to correct errors, suggest new words, and make sure the lines make sense.

This activity is based on the acrostic, where the first letter of every line spells a word.

9.6 Riddles: *I waved and he waved back*

Level Elementary to advanced

Time 30 minutes

Aims To practise vocabulary for describing everyday objects and the jobs they do.

Preparation

Before the lesson choose an everyday household item. For example, *a fridge, a TV, a wardrobe,* which your students can ask 20 questions about.

You could, alternatively, prepare the 'riddle' poems below on the walls as posters.

I think it is a room for hot weather.
I think it is a small house.
Inside I think there are small, dirty stones.

(Potatoes inside a fridge)

Akiko Fujiyoshi

I think there are very small people
Moving in a small box.
I think they can disappear quickly.

(a TV)

Yumiko Inoue

Today I met a friend.
I was so glad I was not alone.

I waved and he waved back
I hugged him but he couldn't
I kissed him but his lips felt cold
I touched him but he felt smooth
I said hello but he didn't reply.

I felt sad	He looked sad
I got angry	He got angry
I shouted	He shouted
I cried	He cried
I hit him	He was broken

(a mirror)

Junko Hozu

Procedure

1 Tell your students that you are an everyday object. Ask them to guess who you are by asking you questions.

   You can only answer yes or no. They can only ask you 20 questions.

   If they get a question right, write the correct statement on the blackboard.

   > You find me in the kitchen.
   > You can open and close me.

2 When they have guessed your object, or when you have four or five statements on the board, stop the questioning. Read the four or five statements through with the students.

   > You find me in the kitchen.
   > You can open and close me.
   > You can put food in me.
   > You can put drinks in me.
   > I'm cold.

3 Explain that the four sentences on the blackboard form a poem called a riddle. The riddle is a guessing game. The poem gives you clues and the reader has to guess what it is about. Now it's their turn to write a riddle!

4 Ask each student to imagine they are an everyday object.
   For a less advanced group, you could choose five or six different words yourself, write them on a label and give them to each group secretly: *computer, radio, microwave oven, mobile phone, TV aerial.*

Ask them to write four or five 'clues', like the ones on the blackboard. Below are some structures your students may find useful.

You find me …	in the on the under the
I can … You can … I am …	

5   After ten minutes invite them to join up with a partner or in a group of three, and read their lines to one another. Can they guess what their partners have written about?

Variation

1   This activity can also be done in teams, as a class competition.

1   Divide the class into groups, or teams, of four or five.
2   Each team must write a riddle about a household object.
3   After ten minutes each group in turn should read out their riddle.
4   The first team to guess the answer wins a point.
5   If no team can guess the riddle, the writers win the point.
6   There could be a small prize for the team that has the most points – a book of riddles, for example!

2   Here is another variation for classes with a wider vocabulary. Give each group specific instructions (secretly):

something found in the bedroom
something found in the kitchen
something found in the yard or garden
something found in the garage

Comments

Riddles are poems in which the writer has a secret. They are often written in the first person singular: *I* … , *I* … , *I* … , *I* … , and it is the reader's task to guess who the *I* is, through the clues in the poem. It is a much-loved form of poetry and the first examples of it in English are over five hundred years old.

Typical errors are:

*   some students write the name of their object in their riddle
*   some students don't give precise enough information and the riddle could describe almost anything! Encourage your students to use precise vocabulary and information, using the dictionary if necessary.

10

Poems as stories:
Go and open the door

Good stories show us characters growing and changing. In a good story, something 'happens'. Even something very small, such as a wine glass falling, or a glimpse of a child on a swing, can be an 'event' if it makes the character change in some way. A good story, too, will show us the character in a context, such as within a family, or dealing with a conflict and it will somehow give us insights into inner and outer lives.

This book has already shown the many poetic ways of recording memories and ideas, by using interesting sounds, rhythms, images, line lengths, shapes on the page. This chapter will invite the student to draw on all these to focus on moments in a story, the moments of change, conflict, recognition, or discovery.

Some of these could be the beginning of longer pieces of story or classroom theatre. These ideas are, indeed, just the beginning of your students 'opening the door' to their own stories.

10.1 First times and last times: *First he was a boy, then he was a man*

Level Lower-intermediate to advanced

Time 25 minutes

Aims To practise describing people. To revise past continuous forms (*she was + -ing*) and to practise talking about time (*in/on/ago*).

Procedure

1 Ask your students to think about a best friend or favourite relative.

Now ask them to go back to their first memory of that person. *Where were they? What was he/she doing?* Ask your students to think hard about that for half a minute, then complete the sentences below.

- *I first saw him/her … (a time)*
- *S/He was … (a place)*
- *S/He was … (an action)*
- *S/He was/had … (a description of him/her)*
- *I thought, ' …'*

2 After five minutes, ask your class to share their sentences with a partner or in a group of three.

3 Now ask the students to think about the most recent memory of that person. Again, ask them to complete the sentences below.
- *I last saw him/her … (a time)*
- *S/He was … (a place)*
- *S/He was … (an action)*
- *S/He was/had … (a description of him/her)*
- *I thought, ' …'*

4 Pairs can read each other's poems, and notice how the friend/relative has changed between the first and second verses.

5 If the class have enjoyed writing these two verses, they can write more sentences of their own to describe what came in between *When we first met* and *When we last met*.

6 Some students may be interested to discuss the poem below: *What has happened between the first and last meeting? Was the writer younger or older than her friend? How do you know?*

> I first saw him where we played
> in the summer holidays.
> He was like me, smooth and thin
> with shorts and freckles.
>
> I last saw him five years later,
> just the same, in the place where we played,
> but this time he had bristles on his chin
> and his voice was lower than before
>
> and I thought,
> 'he's too old to play with me now.'
>
> *French teachers' workshop, Valbonne, France*

Comments

The sentences in this activity will generate the following structures:

I first/last saw him in 1990 (a year)
ten years ago
on a Thursday/1st April (a day of the week, or specific date)
in summer/autumn/March/May (a season or a month)
when s/he was young/old

S/he was _____ (an action). This sentence needs to be completed with the *-ing* form of the verb: *S/he was standing/sitting/laughing/talking/smiling.*

Your students may need help with these different structures.

This activity is about memory, and the process of change. It invites students to think about a person in their lives, and to compare first and last meetings. For some students and some groups, this has been a powerful activity, and has triggered sometimes deep and difficult thoughts. Ways of dealing with this possibility are:

- make sure your group know and trust each other, and invite students at the beginning to work with a friend
- tell the class at the beginning that they do not need to share their poems if they prefer not to.

10.2 Now and then poems: *When I was good*

Level Intermediate to advanced

Time 25 minutes

Aims To focus on high and low moments in one's memories

Procedure

1 Write the following phrases on the blackboard:

When I was bad
When I was good

These phrases are deliberately ambiguous.

Does it mean when I felt bad? or when I behaved badly?
Does it mean when I felt good? or when I behaved well?

Ask your students to interpret the phrases in the way they want to, and to think about:

a a single moment or memory which was 'bad'
b a single moment or memory which was 'good'

Ask them to share information about that moment with a neighbour.

For classes that are not happy with ambiguity, you could give them short titles, instead of phrases:

- *An unhappy moment*
- *A happy moment*
- *A moment when I behaved badly*
- *A moment when I behaved well*

There are endless variations on these titles too:

- *A moment when I was embarrassed*
- *A moment when I was disappointed*
- *A moment when I was surprised*

2 As they talk with their neighbour, invite the students to develop their memory by sharing:

where they were
who else was there
what they did or said

3 Elicit a few examples from the class, by way of comparison and inspiration.

4 When your students are ready, ask them to finish the sentences on the board. They should write at least four or five lines for 'bad' and at least four or five lines for 'good'. If it helps them, they can use the following structures:

When I was good When I was bad	I saw I heard I felt I knew I thought I believed I understood I found I learnt	
but now and now and here I am		

Below is an example you could share:

> When I was good
> I thought I knew everything
> I thought everything was easy
> I thought I was going to be famous
> successful and clever
>
> When I was bad
> I thought I knew nothing
> I thought everything was impossible
> I thought I would never find a job
> or a wife or a house
> or anything to make me happy
>
> *Overseas students' workshop, Nottingham, UK*

5 After 15 minutes, ask your class to reread their lines, and add one more:

but now … !

6 When they are ready, invite them to share their lines with a partner.

Variation

Another phrase which works well with adult groups is:

When I was a child …
But now I …

The poem below is an example:

> When I was a child
> I played by myself in a
> corner of the schoolyard
> all alone.
>
> I hated dolls and I
> hated games, animals were
> not friendly and birds
> flew away.

If anyone was looking
for me I hid behind a
tree and cried out, 'I am
an orphan.'

And here I am, the
center of all beauty!
writing these poems!
Imagine!

Frank O'Hara: from 101 Happy Poems ed. Wendy Cope

10.3 Inner language, outer language: *The music is playing*

Level Lower-intermediate to advanced

This activity has two group tasks:
Group A for less advanced learners
Group B for more fluent learners.

Time 30 minutes

Aims To contrast classroom language with 'inner' language. To contrast controlled language with 'free' language.

Materials

Each group in this activity will need to be given a set of instructions based on the chart outlined under Preparation below.

Group A instructions should be written on a large label and placed in the middle of the table.

> Your topic is *At a party*.
> Your structure is present continuous: *The music is playing.*

Group B instructions should be written on a piece of paper, folded up, and given to a group leader to read quietly to the other group members.

> Write for five minutes whatever comes into your mind on the following topic:
> Walking alone into a crowded room

Preparation

1 Look carefully at the chart below. Select one topic from the first column. Next to it, a language drill is suggested that fits well into this topic, and in the column for Group B a matching 'sub-text' is suggested.

GROUP A Topic	Structure	GROUP B Sub-text
at a party	present continuous *Music is playing*	walking alone into a crowded room
an old friend	used to…	saying goodbye to a loved one
travel arrangements	present simple *the train leaves at 8.00*	taking off in a plane
on holiday	adjectives *the hot sun, the golden sand*	swimming too far out at sea
going to the doctor	question forms: *Does it hurt?*	a scar on my body

Procedure

1   Divide your class into two main groups, group A and group B. If you have a mixed ability group, the A group should be the less fluent learners: the B group should be the more advanced learners.

2   GROUP A
Introduce your group to the topic you have chosen. This group are going to work out at least eight examples/lines/sentences of a language drill, within the chosen topic. For the topic *At a party*, the suggested drill is the present continuous. Your students might generate examples such as:

The women are talking.
The men are drinking beer.
The music is playing.

All examples of the structure which are relevant to the topic are acceptable. The more examples there are the better. A large sub-group can be divided into pairs, each generating their own set of examples.

GROUP B
Members of this group are going to work individually in a quiet space of their own. Give your instructions to this group quietly, so the other group don't hear.
This group is going to explore the 'sub-text'. Introduce them to the sub-text that matches your topic. In the case of *At a party*, this is 'walking alone into a crowded room'. The aim here is fluency: to let ideas and feelings flow unencumbered by concern with accuracy. Incomplete sentences, words and sounds, half phrases and broken rules are all a permissible part of the flow.

Give each group ten minutes to work: group A writing language drills in pairs, group B quietly writing down their thoughts.

3   When ten minutes are over, bring the writing to a close. Regroup the class so that two members of group A work with two members of group B.
    Their task is now to create a 'sandwich' of lines:

    1 line of drill (*We used to go to many parties.*)
    1 line of sub-text (*The stone of apprehension is heavy in my bowels.*)
    1 line of drill
    1 line of sub-text

    and so on, until all students have used up their lines.

4   Invite the groups to rearrange, adjust, revise the lines so they have the most power.

Follow-up

The 'poems' can be performed as classroom theatre. To achieve its full impact, invite each group to prepare a reading in which at least two voices are included: one voice to read the 'text', a second voice to read the 'sub-text'.

Advanced learners may like to take note of the following features:

- the effect of patterns:
  What happens to the 'structure' as it repeats itself through the poem?
  Does the drill acquire a new meaning?
- the emotional impact:
  What happens to the 'sub-text' in contrast with the language drill?
  Does it sound like a second voice? an inner voice? a voice that is never spoken?
  Do the drill and the 'sub-text' begin to echo each other?

Comments

This activity plays with the idea of text and **sub-text**. The text is the language on the surface of things. For example, in the classroom, the text might be the classroom drills and structures being practised. The sub-text is what lies under the surface: what people are really thinking or intending. Woody Allen, in the film *Annie Hall*, made text and sub-text visible. He showed two characters talking to each other: underneath, written at the bottom of the screen, he showed what they were actually thinking.

This activity may seem a little complicated to set up, but you and your students will be surprised at how interesting and compelling the outcome is.

The poem below is an example.

> We used to go to many parties
> *The stone of apprehension heavy in my bowels.*
> We used to organize parties.
> *These smiles I cannot interpret. These fragments of talk I cannot piece together.*
> We used to invite friends and those we loved.
> *The backs I cannot turn. The faces I cannot interpret.*
> We used to decorate the house with yellow flowers.
> *I shrink deeper into myself.*
> We used to be together.
> *Tortoise of anguish – I scuttle for a corner to hide in.*
>
> *Solveiga Ozolina and Alan Maley: Dublin IATEFL workshop*

10.4 Poems about family members

Level Lower-intermediate to advanced

Time 25 minutes

Aims To think about the special roles and tasks of family members.

Procedure

1 Invite your learners to list family members for you, such as *mother, father, brother, cousin, sister, aunt, uncle, brother-in-law,* and write these on the blackboard.

2 With more advanced groups, you could introduce the following poem.

What does it tell us about being a mother?

> Of course I love them, they are my children.
> That is my daughter and this is my son.
> And this is my life I give to please them.
> It has never been used. Keep it safe. Pass it on.
>
> *Anne Stevenson*

3 Choose one of these family members. Ask the group to tell you:
- *what the family member does which is special*
- *what his/her special qualities are*
- *why this kind of family member is important*
- *in what ways this family member is different to all the others*

List their suggestions on the blackboard.

Below are some of the family members and verbs which have been suggested by classes.

A younger brother	talks
An older sister	listens
A mother	never goes away
An aunt	always knows best
An uncle	always thinks they know best
A grandfather	visits on a Sunday
A grandmother	bakes cakes
A cousin	makes tea
A son	shouts
A daughter	is a friend
	remembers
	is important because . . .
	makes you laugh

Here is an example poem:

> A brother can be like a friend.
> You know everything about each other.
> Sometimes this is too much.
> Sometimes you want to forget things.

4 Ask the class to work in groups of three or four. Ask them to agree on one family member they would like to write about. Invite them to share their ideas, and write down the ones they all agree with.

You could also organize your class into self-appointed groups:

- those who wish to write about younger brothers
- those who wish to write about elder sisters etc.

Once the family members are listed on the blackboard, invite students to choose one, and to form a group with others who have made the same choice.

5 After 15 minutes, ask the groups to share their lines with one another.

Follow-up

An interesting follow-up is to ask groups to join their lines and organize them in different ways.

2 lines for mother
2 lines for father
2 lines for mother
2 lines for father

Another interesting follow-up is to ask students now to add adverbs into their sentences: *always, never, sometimes.*

Variation

An interesting variation, which works well with adult groups, is:
Ask each student to list at least two family roles which they play. For
example:

I am a daughter, a sister, and a fiancée
I am a brother, a son, and an uncle

Their task is then to write lines for each of these roles.

Comments

Sometimes students have specific words to describe family members,
which do not exist in English, such as:

- the wife or husband of a cousin
- a brother's wife versus your husband's sister: both are *sister-in-law*
  in English.

Don't worry if your students ask you for a translation of these words
into English. Explain that some relationships do not have specific
descriptions in English. This is an interesting example of cultural
differences.

Some other useful words your students might ask for are:

maternal grandmother/grandfather: your mother's parents
paternal grandmother/grandfather: your father's parents
siblings: brothers and sisters
first cousin once removed: the children of your first cousin, the first
cousins of your parents.

10.5 Family sagas: *My grandmother's bed*

Level   Lower-intermediate to advanced

Time   30 minutes

Aims   To capture aspects of time and place in a few lines. To practise the
simple past for telling simple narratives.

Preparation

Check **saga** in the glossary.

Procedure

1   Write the following three family names on the blackboard:

> grandmother/grandfather
> mother/father
> me

Ask the students what they notice about these names. What do they
think about them?

Give them two minutes to talk to a partner about any thoughts which emerge, looking at these names.

2   Now explain you are going to think about these family members through one everyday household item that is typical of them.

What everyday item would this be?
It could be a piece of clothing, a piece of furniture, or a part of the house or garden.

Invite them to think about this, and share their idea with their partner. Some that have been suggested include:

a hat	*a pipe*	*a pair of spectacles*
the garden	*the bed*	*the balcony*

3   Write some of the suggestions on the blackboard and invite your students to explain why they have chosen these items.

4   Now ask each student to choose one everyday item from the blackboard or from the earlier discussion.

Ask them to think about this everyday item and how it was for three generations in the family:

my grandfather's hat: a flat felt cap
my father's hat: a handkerchief tied at each corner to keep off the sun
my hat: a baseball cap

Grandma's garden: a yard with chickens
Mother's garden: a green lawn in the suburb with cherry trees
my garden: a balcony in the town with flowerpots

At this stage, if the student's selected item is inappropriate for the comparison (for example, their grandfather smoked a pipe, but neither they nor their father do), ask them to change the item, so it becomes something shared by all three generations.

Below is an example of a poem about three generations of beds. You could share this with your students as an example.

> My grandmother's bed –
> monumental and dark;
> a soft mattress, pink flowered eiderdown,
> crisp sheets;
> rubber and lucozade hot-water bottles.
>
> My mother's bed –
> the best orthopaedic;
> nylon sheets, diaries and duvets,
> electrically heated –
> snoring husband in the next room.
>
> My bed –
> cobbled together from old divans and shawls,
> made up nightly
> for cats and me to pile into,
> dream diary to hand.
>
> *Annys Blackwell, Plymouth poetry workshop*

5   Now your class have 15 minutes to write:

lines describing the everyday item as it was for a grandparent
lines describing the everyday item as it was for a parent
lines describing the everyday item as it is now

6   After 15 minutes, ask the groups to share their lines with one another.

Variations

Some students in this activity have wished to write about:

- *a parent*
- *themselves*
- *a son or daughter*

This also works very well, and can be offered as a choice for those who do have sons and daughters they wish to write about.

There are also more structured variations of this activity earlier in this book: 5.1 – Being young, being old; 8.4 – Diary poems: First pair of high heels; 10.1 – First times and last times.

Comments

The descriptions do not need to be sentences. Your students could also write key words, impressions, or thoughts. Allow all possibilities which communicate to others.

10.6 Poems about changes: *First I was, Then I was*

Level   Lower-intermediate to advanced

Time   20 minutes

Aims   To describe change and growth. To practise the simple past.

Procedure

1   Write the following phrases on the blackboard, and ask your students what the link is between each group of words.

> seed flower
> river sea
> baby child man/woman
> caterpillar butterfly

Here are some possible answers:

- One becomes the other
- One grows into the other
- One changes into the other.

2 Ask the students if they can suggest other pairs of words that describe the same thing. Write their suggestions on the blackboard.

3 When you have several other examples on the board, write the two sentences:

First I was …
Then I was …

Ask your students to finish these sentences. Below are some further suggestions, which you could offer as examples.

water	steam	air
bud	blossom	fruit
cotton	cloth	
wood	paper	book
mountain	rock	grain of sand

First I was wood
Then I was coal

First I was coal
Then I was fire

First I was fire
Then I was air

First I was a spring
Then I was an ocean

First I was a seed
Then I was a sunflower

First I was a bud
Then I was a blossom
Then I was a cherry
Then I was a pie

Plymouth poetry workshop

4   Now divide your class into groups of two and three. Ask the students to write pairs of sentences like these, using their ideas or those on the blackboard as a starting point.

5   After ten minutes, invite the groups to share their ideas.

Follow-up

Another variation could be the contrast between simple past and simple present forms:

• *First I was …*
• *Now I am …*

Comments

Many of the nouns do not require an article, for example:

water, steam, cotton, cloth, wool

This is because they are general and uncountable words.

Some of the nouns which are specific, concrete, and countable will need an article:

specific animals: a sheep
specific fruit: an apple
specific flowers: a sunflower

10.7   A visualization poem: *Go and open the door*

Level   **Lower-intermediate to advanced**

Time   **20 minutes**

Aims   **To raise morale if the group have become unhappy. To practise modals (*it may/might/could*). To practise the structure *Go and …* + verb in its root or unchanged form (*go and see, go and answer, go and open …*).**

Procedure

1   Explain to your students that you are going to take them on a journey. At each point in the journey, they will be asked to write a few lines, so they need to have with them a piece of paper and a pen.

2   When your class are ready and quiet, read through the visualization below, or use it as a basis for your own 'script'. You might want to make it simpler, or to adapt it, so it fits into your own classroom. The script below is short and can fit into a 20-minute part of the lesson. You also may wish to make it much longer. See the Variations below for other possibilities.

3   At different points in the script, you are going to stop and invite your students to write. These places are clearly marked. There are a few 'stage directions' which you do not read aloud. These appear in brackets.

A secret door has been found in this classroom. It's never been found before. It's a large oak door, and it's hidden in the wall. (Say where in your classroom.)

Usually the door is locked, but today you are able to open the door and go through it. Think about the door and where it is.
Now write down:

Go and open the door.

Now write down what there might be through the door.
You can begin:

There might be
There may be
Maybe there is

(Wait five minutes for your class to write.)

When you are ready, you go towards the door and find the handle.

You turn the handle and the door opens easily.

Inside is a room. You walk round the room, and you are amazed: all the things you see are from your childhood and from all the places you have visited and lived in since then. It is as if you have been storing things in this room all your life.

Now write down what you can see in the room.

(Wait five minutes for your class to write.)

You know that all these things must stay in the room, for your next visit.

You look round and round the room, picking things up, remembering them.

Then you decide you are going to take just one thing away with you as a memory.

You stand in the middle of the room thinking. What shall I take? This – or that? Or that?

Then you choose your one object.

You go up to it, pick it up, think about it. Yes, this is the object you will take with you. Now write down what that object is.

(Wait one minute for your class to write down their object.)

You hold it tightly in your hand, and come back through the door.

You close the door behind you. You will go back through the door another day.

Then you come back into the classroom, and quietly walk back to your desk.

4   After half a minute of quiet, ask your students to turn to their neighbour and tell them what their object was and why they chose it.

5 Now give the class five minutes to look at the lines they have written, and to add or change them. After this time, invite them to share their lines with a neighbour.

Variations

If you would like to make the 'journey' longer, you could extend it, and opportunities for writing, with further stages:

You walk through the door, and suddenly you see/hear/smell …
You walk further, and after a few minutes you meet …
You ask him/her the question you've always wanted to ask: …
He/she answers: …

You can, of course, develop the journey in any way you wish or feel inspired to, as long as there are 'writing breaks' for your students to interact with the story.

The poem builds up, simply with the key words and phrases the students write down at each break. Here are examples generated by a pre-intermediate general English class in Plymouth.

> Go and open the door.
> There may be a lot of
> friendly people.
> If there's noise, it'll disappear soon.
> Even if there's only a dead leaf.
>
> At least there'll be
> A star
>
> *Akiko Fujiyoshi: General English class*
>
> Go and open the door.
> Maybe outside there's spring.
> A beautiful field and
> A lovely bench which
> I can sit on with someone.
>
> Go and open the door.
> If there are ghosts
> and darkness
> it will go away.
>
> Go and open the door.
> Even if there are only
> Fallen leaves
> Go and open the door.
>
> At least
> There'll be lovely
> Memories.
>
> *Kaori Hashizume: General English class*

Follow-up

This activity was inspired by the following poem by the Czech poet Miroslav Holub. You might like to share and discuss this with your class.

> Go and open the door.
>   Maybe outside there's
>   A tree, or a wood,
> A garden,
> Or a magic city.
>
> Go and open the door.
>   Maybe a dog's rummaging.
>   Maybe you'll see a face,
> Or an eye
> Or the picture
>   Of a picture.
>
> Go and open the door.
>   If there's a fog
>   It will clear.
>
> Go and open the door.
>   Even if there's only
>   The darkness ticking,
>   Even if there's only
>   The hollow wind,
>   Even if
>   Nothing
>   Is there,
> Go and open the door.
>
> At least
> There'll be
> A draught.
>
> *Miroslav Holub*

Appendix 1

Poetry forms

There are several poetry forms which we have not covered in detail in this book, because they are dealt with well elsewhere. Below are short descriptions of these. For classes from intermediate to advanced, they may form exciting models for further experiments with poetry.

1 Poems which count syllables

Haiku

Haiku is a form of verse from Japan. Arthur Waley translated many haiku into English and made them popular.

The essence of a haiku is that it captures a tiny moment in nature: for example, the moment a feather falls, or a bird alights on a branch, or the sun lights up a drop of water. Its content is about tiny changes, and its form is, as a result, tiny.

Pure haiku are 17 syllables long.

Line	Syllable
1	5
2	7
3	5

One of the great masters of haiku was a poet who called himself Basho and lived in a hut next to a banana tree.

> On the lily pad
> a frog jumps: the old, still pond,
> the sound of water.

However, many modern haiku keep the spirit of the Japanese, but change the number of syllables used:

> The tulip drops its red
> Leaf to earth.
> Spring ends.

Or change the subject matter and use it humorously:

Basho reads poems to his wife:
Nothing important
Can be done in seventeen
Syllables, she said

Keith Harrison, from *The Complete Basho poems*

Tanka are sequences of haiku, each joined by two extra lines. The extra lines complete the haiku that went before, and prepare for the next haiku. There are usually seven syllables each.

Cinquain

Cinquains are patterns of line length. The length of the line is calculated by the number of syllables.

The word comes from 'cinq' – meaning five in French. There are five lines in a cinquain:

Line	Number of syllables
1	2
2	4
3	6
4	8
5	2

The effect of the cinquain is of an idea growing and then ebbing away again.

If you draw lines around a cinquain, you will have a diamond.

Autumn
leaves become brown
falling floating twirling
all awash in icy puddles
Autumn

classrooms
on a Friday
wind throwing leaves about
water rushing down the plughole
Fridays

Jane Spiro

To find out more about about haiku, look at the following website: www.toyomasu.com/haiku/

2 Poems which repeat lines

Refrain

A refrain is a line, or part of a line, or a group of lines, which is repeated throughout a poem. The line may be changed very slightly, but it keeps returning in the poem until the reader is familiar with it. The repetitions are interesting, because often they appear to change in meaning, and take on a new significance after each repetition.

Your learners can experiment with writing refrains for their own poems.

They can:
- choose a line from the poem that they like, and after each verse, repeat their chosen line

or
- repeat their chosen line at the beginning of each verse.

Here is an example from Activity 10.7:

> Deep breath and open your eyes
> Perhaps forward there's a problem or
> A maze or a crowded city
>
> Deep breath and open your eyes
> Perhaps people smiling. Perhaps you'll see
> A truth or a lie or lovely sunshine.
>
> Deep breath and open your eyes
> If there's darkness, it will be bright.
>
> Deep breath and open your eyes.
> Even if there's only the ocean waving,
> even if there's only the wide grass
>
> Deep breath and open your eyes
> There may be something nice.
>
> *Alice Wang Hsiu-Li*

3 Poems with special rhyme schemes

Rhyming couplet

A couplet is two lines of poetry which rhyme and which have a similar number of syllables. Shakespearean sonnets are most remembered for the rhyming couplet in the final two lines.

A couplet can be a complete poem all on its own: or it can be the 'punchline' ending of a longer poem. Here is a rhyming couplet from Activity 1.4:

When you feel   heart
When I hurt   part

Limerick

The limerick is a very popular poetic form, but it has not been included in detail here because it is a very difficult one to imitate well. However, your students may wish to have a try, and if so, these are the rules to follow:

Limericks are five lines long with two rhymes:
Rhyme 1 in lines 1, 2, and 5
Rhyme 2 in lines 3 and 4

The lines are also often regular in length.

Line	Number of syllables	Rhyme
1	8	A
2	8	A
3	5 or 6	B
4	5 or 6	B
5	8	A

Edward Lear (1812–1888) was the most famous writer of limericks, and made them popular in the 19th century. They are still a favourite form of humour today.

> There was an Old Man with a beard,
> Who said, 'It is just as I feared! –
> Two Owls and a Hen,
> four Larks and a Wren,
> Have all built their nests in my beard!'

> *Edward Lear*

Ballad

The ballad is a poem that tells a story. Often ballads echo the history of a people, events in a culture. Ballads can be a metaphor for the loss of a country, or a war, or the migration of a people. They were often read aloud, or sung to a lute or mandolin.

They are usually written in verses (or stanzas) of four lines each, with a simple rhyme scheme:

A		A
B	or	A
C		B
B		B

Many ballads, too, have a chorus which repeats alternately after every verse.

Below is the opening of the ballad *The Owl and the Pussycat*. Notice that the rhyme scheme follows the pattern A/B/C/B.

> The owl and the pussycat went to sea
> In a beautiful pea-green boat.
> They took some honey and plenty of money
> Wrapped up in a five pound note.

Epitaph

An epitaph is about someone who has died, but it is often short, with a rhyme scheme, and can be humorous. The typical rhyme scheme for humorous epitaphs is A B A B: but the important rhyme needs to be in the last line.

An epitaph is traditionally written on a tombstone, but many poets have written 'mock' epitaphs, beginning with the phrase: Here lies …

For example:

> Here lies the Bionic Man
> His battery, it did cease.
> His working days are over
> May he rust in peace.
> Anon.

4 Poems which have special rhythms

Rap

Afro-Caribbean poets and musicians developed a style that was halfway between poem and song. The poems are designed to be read aloud, with a strong beat, which you can dance to, click your fingers to, or drum to. The poet who made rap popular to a Western audience, was Linton Kwesi Johnson.

5 Poems which have a special mood

Elegy

The elegy both mourns and praises the loved one. Elton John's song 'Candle in the Wind' was an elegy for Princess Diana (and before that, for Marilyn Monroe). Many of the great poets wrote famous elegies for friends and lovers who died young, for example, Milton, Tennyson, Keats, Hopkins.

But the elegy need not only be about the passing of a person: it could mourn the passing of anything that is loved – a favourite season, a tree being cut down, a building being knocked down, a city that has been bombed.

An elegy includes descriptions, feelings, reflections on loss. There is no set structure to the rhymes or rhythms of an elegy: it is the content and mood which matters.

Appendix 2

Glossary of key words

A

Abstract nouns may be an idea, thought or philosophy. We cannot see or touch an abstract noun. Sometimes abstract nouns end like this: *-hood, -ness, -ism*. For example: *childhood, happiness, capitalism*. They cannot usually change into the plural by adding an *-s*. Also, we usually use abstract nouns without an article: *the* or *a*.

Adjectives are usually found in front of or near nouns, to describe them and give information about them. Adjectives cannot change into the plural. Some typical endings which help us to recognize adjectives are: *-y, -ful, -less*.

Alliteration is the repetition of the first sounds in words – usually consonant sounds. The repetition of sounds can create strong musical effects: for example, *Willow whistle-in-the-wind*. For this reason, poets like using alliteration, and so do businesses trying to sell products – because we remember more easily a name which alliterates.

Antonyms are words which are opposites. Some words have exact opposites: for example, *happy* and *sad*, *tall* and *short*. Some words have opposites which are shown grammatically, such as *powerful: powerless*. Other words do not have exact opposites, for example, *shy*. There are several possible opposites here: *confident, loud, friendly*.

Assonance is the resemblance of sound between two syllables in nearby words. The rhyming may be from two or more accented vowels, but not consonants, e.g. *tilting, windmills*. Or the use of identical consonants, e.g. *killed, cold*.

C

Calligrams are shapes made from a single word, to illustrate its meaning. The actual shape and form of the letters represents the meaning of the word.

fat   grow up

Chain poems are a form in which the last word of each line becomes the first word of the next line.
Another variation of the chain poem happens when the last line of a verse becomes the first line of the next verse.

Clauses have a main verb in them, which will give us information about person and time. For example: *The spider ate the ant* is a clause. We know the spider did the eating, and that it was in the past. *Eating ants* is not a clause: who does the eating this time, and when?

Collocations are groups of words which belong together. Sometimes words come in pairs. If the words are separated, or joined with another new word, they can sound strange.
For example:
We say Merry Christmas, but not Merry birthday

Complex sentences have at least two clauses.
The main clause will have a verb that gives information about time and person. The second clause will be attached to the first, with a link word such as: *that, while, although, where, why*.

Concrete nouns describe things which we can touch, feel, and see. Rain, trees, toast, and tigers are all concrete nouns.

Concrete poems are poems set out on the page in unusual formations that reflect their meaning. The way the poem looks on the page is part of its message.
For example, Wes McGee wrote a poem in the shape of Africa, and Lewis Carroll wrote a poem in the shape of a cat's long tail.

Connotation is the 'feeling' of a word – whether it appears to say something good or bad, or whether it has a positive or negative sense to it.

Consonant clusters happen when groups of consonants sit next to each other in a word. For example, *snorts* has got a consonant cluster at the beginning: *s n*; and a consonant cluster at the end: *r t s*.

Co-ordinate clauses are joined together using the conjunctions *and, but, or*. Each co-ordinate clause in a sentence is equally important, and has a main verb in it.

Countable nouns are words which can be counted. You can't, for example, count *milk*, but you can count bottles, or glasses of milk. Bottles and glasses are countable, milk is not. Countable nouns usually:
• need an article in the singular (*a* or *the*)
• can be described either in the singular or the plural.

E

Exclamations are one- or two-word phrases followed by an exclamation mark (!). They are acceptable as complete sentences. They do not need a verb or any other structure to be complete. For this reason, they are very useful for beginners. Examples are, *Oh! Yes! OK!*

F

Free verse allows poets to choose to use rhymes when and if they want to, to make lines as long or as short as they want, and to make the content whatever suits.

This does not mean free verse is easy. To make it interesting, the poet must still make language as powerful as possible, by using interesting sounds, rhythms, images, line lengths, shapes on the page.

Found poems are words or phrases that have been plucked out of everyday life, and placed on the page, just as a pebble from the beach may be placed in a museum case, or a leaf from a tree may be placed in a picture frame. What happens to these objects in their strange new surroundings is that we look at them freshly and carefully. We notice how interesting the words of the list might be; how rich or surprising the ideas are sitting next to one another on the paper. This kind of poem is called a found poem, because it has been 'found' and borrowed from the everyday world. It is something your students will be able to do too, as they become more confident with the language.

G

Genre Lists, memos, application forms, diaries, letters, recipes, postcards are all genres, or text types. We can recognize them from the way they are set out on the page, the length of lines, the choice of words and structures. For example, a list will probably be in a long thin line, with words on their own rather than in structures or in sentences. A picture postcard is likely to be informal and friendly, with special formulae for opening or closing. Knowing the features of a genre can help learners to write more precisely to match their audience and purpose.

I

Idioms are short phrases or expressions which have come to be used regularly in the language. Their meaning can often not be guessed just from the parts of the phrase, but they are understood as part of the culture. For this reason, idioms are particularly difficult for language learners, and yet they are the very thing that makes a learner feel they have joined the language community. They are best learnt as 'chunks' rather than dividing them up into parts, which often do not make sense separately. For example: *as pleased as Punch, to hit the nail on the head.*

Imperatives are ways of commanding, giving orders, or instructions. For example:

See!
Go!
Run!

Infinitives are verbs in their unchanged form. Infinitives can be with or without *to* and they do not give us any information about person or time. The infinitive without *to* is often called the **root**.

(to) read
(to) go
(to) stop
(to) leave

Interrogative is the grammatical term for questions. The interrogative, or question form, is made by:

- Reversing the subject and verb: *Are you there? Is he happy? Are you coming?*
- Adding the auxiliary *do* + the unchanged root of the verb: *Do you like it? Does it hurt?*
- Using a question word: *Who, what, where, when, how*

L

Lexical sets are words which all belong to the same topic. For example: *mother, brother, aunt, sister, cousin* all belong to the lexical set of the family. Research has shown that it is much easier to learn new vocabulary when we meet it in lexical sets, rather than individually.

M

Metaphors transform one thing into another. The word *metaphor* comes from the Greek meaning 'to transform' or 'to change'. There is no phrase such as 'like' or 'as if' to suggest there is a comparison, but the objects in a metaphor change and become something else.

> *My mother is a lake*
> *I see my face in her.*
> (Activity 3.2)
>
> *Hope is a spoon*
> *Love is jazz.*
> (Activity 3.5)

Mini-sagas are a recognized form, in which a story is told in 50 words. A mini-saga often has a clear beginning, middle, and end, just like in a longer story.

Modals are verbs such as *can, could, might, may, should*. These verbs are not complete on their own, but need another to complete their sense. They are unusual because they have many different meanings. They are also unusual because they do not change their form when used with different pronouns.

Morphemes are the parts of words which have a grammatical function. The following are examples of morphemes:

-ly = an adverb
-ing = the present participle of a verb
-s = the plural ending of a noun

O

Onomatopoeia is a term used to describe words that contain sounds similar to the noises they describe. Examples of onomatopoeic words in English are:
crash! plop! clunk!

P

Paradoxes happen when two opposite ideas or situations exist side by side. They can be expressed by phrases such as:
Dark with excessive bright thy skirts appear (Milton)
Who never said a foolish thing
And never did a wise one
(Rochester about Charles II)

Personification happens when something that is not human, or not even living, is described as if it is human and alive.
For example: 'the storm roars like a horse'.

Praise-song is part of the practice of wild and joyful compliments for leaders, beloved objects, and beloved people. Traditionally the praise-song would have been danced, with beating drums and gorgeous costumes to accompany the words.

Prefixes are syllables which fit on to the beginning of words, and which can change their meaning. Usually these syllables have a specific meaning, which they give to any word they attach to.
For example: *re-* again   *reread* – to read again   *repeat* – to do something again

Proper nouns are the names of people or places. You can recognize them because they start with a capital letter.

R

Relative clauses are attached to sentences with relative pronouns, such as: *why, who, when*. For example, *what* here marks the beginning of the relative clause.
I wonder what makes her sad

Relative pronouns are the words which link two clauses and which refer back to information in the first part of the sentence. *Who, what, why, which* are all relative pronouns.

Rhyme words have the same last vowel sound and consonant sound. For example: *cat, hat, pat*.

Riddles are poems in which the writer has a secret. They are often written in the first person singular *I* and it is the reader's task to guess who the *I* is, through the clues in the poem. It is a much-loved form of poetry, and the first examples of it in English are over five hundred years old.

Roots are the form of verb without any changes and without the 'to'. For example: *go, talk, see, read*. They are the part of the verb we use to create other forms. For example: *talk + ing; talk + ed; talk + s*.

S

Sagas are long stories that take place over several generations.

Similes compare two things in a way which is surprising and interesting. A good simile will make us think about both things in a new way. The comparison will be introduced either by: *like* or by *as*.
For example:
Rain 'clutters along the roofs,
Like the tramp of hoofs' (Henry Wadsworth Longfellow)

Subordinate clauses are joined to the main clause with conjunctions such as *while, although, when, if, that*. A subordinate clause is not complete on its own. It is attached to a main clause, and needs this to complete its meaning.

Sub-text is the 'hidden' meaning which lies underneath what people actually say or write. For example: the teacher *says*: 'Let's leave that last question for homework', but what she *thinks* is: 'I've had enough! I want to go home!' These words in her head are the sub-text.

Suffixes are the syllables which fit on to the end of a word, and which change their meaning or function in the sentence.
-ful changes a word into an adjective, with a positive meaning (full of).
-less changes a word into an adjective with a negative meaning (without).
Both of these are suffixes.

U

Uncountable nouns cannot be divided up and counted. *Sky* can't be counted, neither can *sugar, milk, water*. All these are uncountable. They cannot go into the plural.

Further reading

1 Collections of short poems for the classroom

Bates, M. (ed.) 1999. *Poetry as a Foreign Language.* Edinburgh: White Adder Press.

A collection of poems gathered together from learners, teachers, and 'visiting experts', in response to the first Poetry in EFL competition. This has a useful index at the back, classifying poems into themes and topics, and is the only anthology of its kind, representing the voices of learners themselves.

Benson, G., J. Chernaik, and H. Cicely (eds.) 1992. *Poems on the Underground.* London: Cassell.

Short poems which are funny, sad, wise and thought-provoking. Many are remarkably (and deceptively) simple. These could be used and enjoyed with adult classes of all levels.

Cope, W. (ed.) 2001. *Heaven on Earth: 101 Happy Poems.* London: Faber and Faber.

A happy, optimistic collection of poems, many of which could readily be understood by groups of students from intermediate level and beyond.

Heath R.B. (ed.) 1993. *Tradewinds.* Harlow: Longman.

A multicultural anthology of poems from China, India, the Caribbean, Africa, with short explanations, activities and illustrations. An interesting and teacher-friendly collection.

Nichols, G. 1996. *Can I Buy a Slice of Sky?* London: Hodder Children's Books.

A delightful collection of short and reader-friendly poems which suggest many possibilities for imitation and exploitation, and would appeal to children.

2 Resource books for teachers

Carter, R. and M. Long. 1987. *The Web of Words.* Cambridge: Cambridge University Press.

A practical resource book aimed at upper-intermediate to advanced students, exploiting short literary texts in the language classroom, using a wide range of communicative task types.

Collie J. and S. Slater. 1987. *Literature in the Language Classroom.* Cambridge: Cambridge University Press.

Practical activities showing how texts, including complete novels, can be used as the starting point for student interaction, activities, and projects.

Graham, C. 1983. *Jazz Chants.* Oxford: Oxford University Press.

English rhythms practised through exciting chanted drills that are close to rap, and which set up an irresistible class dynamic.

Hall, E., C. Hall and A. Leech. 1990. *Scripted Fantasy in the Classroom.* London: Routledge Education.

This book takes the teacher step by step through the stages of building up visualization and fantasy in the classroom. If you enjoy the visualization activity in Activity 10.7, this book will give you many other scripts which you can use with your classes.

Holmes, V. and M.R. Moulton. 2001. *Writing Simple Poems.* Cambridge: Cambridge University Press.

25 short, practical, and workable activities for creating poetry in the language classroom. There is a focus on language across the curriculum, and language taught in schools, but many of the activities would work with students of all ages.

Maley, A. and A. Duff. 1989. *The Inward Ear.* Cambridge: Cambridge University Press.

Lively communicative writing tasks suitable for learners at all levels.

Matthews, P. 1996. *Sing me the Creation.* Stroud: Hawthorn Press.

Designed for creative-writing workshops in native-speaker contexts, but many are adaptable for the foreign-language classroom too: over 300 short activities for individual and group work in creative writing.

Morgan J. and M. Rinvolucri. 1983. *Once upon a Time.* Cambridge: Cambridge University Press.

Story activities for the language classroom.

Parkinson B. and H. Reid Thomas. 2000. *Teaching Literature in a Second Language.* Edinburgh: Edinburgh University Press.

Considers not only literary texts which learners might read and appreciate, but also the voices of learners and teachers in response to them.

3 Articles and discussions about poetry in the classroom

Hess, N. 2003. 'Real language through poetry: a formula for making meaning' *ELT Journal* 57: 19–25.

McConachie, J. and H. Sage 'Since feeling is first: thoughts on sharing poetry in the ESOL classroom.' *English Teaching Forum* 23/1

Tomlinson, B. 1986. 'Using Poetry with Mixed Ability Language Classes' *ELT Journal* 37/1

4 Useful websites for poetry

www.gigglepotz.com/kidspoetry.htm
Short, fun, and funny poems usable in the classroom. Designed for children but adult language learners will enjoy it too.

www.greenmountainclub.org/ACTSoundPoems.htm
A resource list and activity ideas for using and writing sound poetry with children.

www.poets.org
Poetry news, events, and links to other poetry websites.

www.onlinepoetryclassroom.org/how
Poetry units based on the poetry national curriculum, but usable in a much wider range of contexts.

www.toyomasu.com/haiku/
A site dedicated to haiku with writing activities, definition, and lots of examples, both old and modern.

http://wings.buffalo.edu/epc
E-poetry, news, and resources, articles and poetry events to keep the teacher in touch with the poetry world.

You can also visit the website for this book:
http://www.oup.com/elt/teacher/rbt

5 Dictionaries and reference books

The suggestions below supplement the students' dictionaries and 'activators' you might already have in the class library. They include thesauri and dictionaries for developing word power, synonyms and antonyms, rhymes, idioms, cultural information, and historical information about words.

Basic English Thesaurus 2002. London: Peter Collin Publishing.

Designed for pre-intermediate to intermediate learners to develop their word power, by finding synonyms. There are clear definitions and sample sentences for each headword and set of synonyms.

Espy, W.R. (ed.) 1986. *Words to Rhyme With*: *For Poets and Song Writers.* London: Macmillan.

Fergusson, R. (ed.) 1983. *Penguin Dictionary of Proverbs.* London: Penguin Books.

Flavell L. and R. Flavell. 1995. *Dictionary of Word Origins.* London: Kyle Cathie Limited.
Short, interesting, and surprising descriptions of the history of everyday words and idioms.

Green J. 1999. *English Thesaurus for Students.* London: Bloomsbury.
Over 4,000 terms arranged under 400 main headwords to extend word power.

Hoad T.F. 1993. *The Concise Oxford Dictionary of Etymology.* Oxford: Oxford University Press.
Brief, useful descriptions of the history and origins of words.

Longman Dictionary of English Language and Culture. New Edition 1998. Harlow: Longman.
A dictionary uncovering the cultural story behind names of people, places, and events.

Index